What People Are Say

Freedom Sailors is a story of sheer courage and fortitude, written and edited by the very people who lived it. The book chronicles a remarkable chapter of history, where civil society memorably triumphed over the Israeli military machine, as it laid an unforgiving siege on the 1.5 million inhabitants of Gaza.

As 'spooks' lurked around, and military men declared war on two small boats, 44 civil society activists carried out an audacious act that fundamentally altered the nature of international solidarity with the Palestinians.

This book must be read and read again, not only as a tribute to those who proved that 'ordinary people' can achieve extraordinary feats, but because it details an experience that must be carefully studied and widely discussed.

Free Gaza challenged the outrageous 'routine' where Palestinians are often left alone in their conflict with US-supported and financed Israel. It was that supposedly short, but extremely arduous sea journey that has finally opened up a world of possibilities for entire communities around the world to stand in active solidarity with the Palestinian people.

This is not just the story of how two tiny boats challenged the illegal Israeli siege on Gaza, but a vivid description of how a small group of people forever changed the rules of the game.

A riveting account. A must read.

Ramzi Baroud, *Palestine Chronicle*, Born and Raised in Gaza and Author of *My Father Was a Freedom Fighter*

The un-missable story of the first sea journey to break the siege of Gaza, which was to launch an international trend. Reads like a super thriller, but with a noble and enduring morality at its core. A moving exposition of the heroism of ordinary people pitted against injustice. A must read for those who want to understand Israel and the Palestinians.

Ghada Karmi, Palestinian Doctor of Medicine, Author and Academic

You cannot read this story and not be moved to tears at the tremendous ongoing suffering, under Israeli occupation, of the Palestinian people of Gaza. (Something I witnessed myself when I visited Gaza on the Free Gaza boat 'Dignity' in October, 2008.) But at the same time, your spirits will be uplifted and you will be deeply inspired by this story of the vision, courage, and sacrifice of some brave hearts who started the Free Gaza Movement, because they lived out the words of the late Vittorio Arrigoni and remembered to 'stay human'. Out of such a spirit of nonviolent love in action arises not only the hope for Palestinian freedom, but for humanity itself.

Mairead Maguire, Nobel Peace Laureate, Co-Founder Peace People, Northern Ireland

This is a moving story of principled, courageous people going to the aid of the people of Gaza, whose suffering and resistance pass responsibility to all of us to take action. Those who took up this challenge and sailed to Gaza offer a vivid example of how and why we should stand up to injustice and corrupt power.

John Pilger, Journalist and Filmmaker

When something is profoundly wrong, and governments won't take action, then people of conscience lead the way. This is the story of a group of such people who organised boats from Cyprus to break the siege of Gaza. It is moving and heartwarming, and worth reading; because it reminds us, that it is through such actions, alongside the struggles of the Palestinian people, that justice will come to Palestine.

Right Honorable Clare Short, Former UK MP and Minister for International Development

I sailed with the second Free Gaza boat accompanied by other politicians and activists and loaded to the gunnels with essential medical supplies. It was like a Mediterranean cruise compared with the first sailing of the good boats *Free Gaza* and *Liberty*.

This story of energy, enterprise and a refusal to give up ranks with many of the great adventure stories of history, not least because the threat of action by the Israelis was ever present and eventually realized, with the brutal attack and murders on the Freedom Flotilla in May 2010.

This book MUST be read by people who care about freedom and justice.

Baroness Jenny Tonge, House of Lords, UK

This was such a moving experience! Humanity is desperately ill; what is the cure? It is the medicine of solidarity, with any of us who are in peril. That is the message of this deeply moving and important book about the first voyage to break the illegal Israeli siege of Gaza. Reading like a fast-paced action movie, it moves us to tears, to smiles, to sadness, to consciousness . . . hopefully to action.

We *are* Humanity's keeper . . . whether in sadistically brutalized Gaza, the largest prison in the world or in any of a thousand places on our beleaguered earth. Most of all it demonstrates how we humans, with all our limitations, our frailties and fears and bouts of irrational joy and craziness are still capable of standing up for what is right, of seeing each other clearly as worthy of the profoundest caring; of being the ones who, no matter what, do not turn away.

Alice Walker, Earthling Poet, Writer, and Human Rights Activist

Freedom Sailors

The inside story of the Free Gaza movement's first voyage to challenge Israel's illegal blockade of Gaza, and how we succeeded in spite of ourselves

Boats sailed 1900 KM (1200 miles)
Another 386 KM (240 miles) to reach Gaza

Edited by Greta Berlin and Bill Dienst, M.D.
Copyright 2012 Greta Berlin and Bill Dienst
ISBN: 9780615654898

This book is available in print at most online retailers. Copies may also be ordered at www.FreedomSailors.com

Free Gaza and Liberty arriving in Gaza port accompanied by Gaza fishermen.

Front cover courtesy of Independent MP Jamal El-Khoudary, Gaza Illustration on back page courtesy of Carlos Latuff

Table of Contents

Dedication

This book is dedicated to the Palestinians of Gaza; as well as those living in present-day Israel, the occupied West Bank, and in the Palestinian diaspora. You will never be forgotten!

We look forward to the day all Palestinians will be granted their basic human rights – rights that include the freedom to travel, go to work and educate their children. Many of these rights are denied to the people of Gaza and to many Palestinians in the occupied West Bank.

The majority of the Royalties earned from this book will be donated to Gaza- based humanitarian organizations as directed through the Gaza Community Mental Health Programme (GCMHP). By purchasing this book, you will be contributing directly toward helping people living in Gaza. A small portion of the book sales will also go to help activists return to Gaza. The authors of this book will receive no royalties.

And we dedicate this book to the fallen members of our movement, members who gave their lives for justice: Riad Hamad, died in 2008, Vittorio Arrigoni, killed in Gaza in 2011, Scott Kennedy, died in 2011

Preface

Freedom Sailors is a much-needed account of how a small group of ordinary people conceived and executed what seemed like a grandiose and audacious plan to break Israel's illegal military blockade of the Gaza Strip, a blockade that keeps more than 1.5 million people in an open-air prison. Knowing what we know now — that Israel Defense Forces would later murder nine people, including an unarmed American citizen, Furkan Dogan, executed at point-blank range during a later Freedom Flotilla — our chutzpah is astonishing.

During the Israeli assault on Lebanon in 2006, a small group of people decided to sail boats across the Mediterranean to break a vicious and illegal blockade on 1.5 million people trapped in Gaza, a small slice of beachfront property squeezed between Israel and Egypt. We were worried that, with the attention of the world on Lebanon, Israel would begin another round of dispossession in Palestine, especially in Gaza. In a little over two years, we raised the money to purchase two dilapidated fishing boats stored in secret ports in Greece, collected 44 passengers, crew and journalists, aged 22 to 81 and chose Cyprus as our embarkation point. Although a small contingent of passengers and crew sailed from Greece with the boats, most of the passengers waited in Cyprus.

We were a small group of idealists who had big ideas but little understanding of what we were doing. Had we really understood the dangers, we might not have gone ahead. Maybe we would have, but we truly were amateurs - most of us had never even been on a boat. Before we sailed, one of our coordinators told us: "If you aren't willing to face attack, injury, imprisonment or death, don't get on the boat."

Everyone got on the boats.

People who weren't there or weren't close to us may not realize just how isolated we were once we finally set sail to

Gaza on the late morning of August 22, 2008; over 33 hours on the sea, no internet, and only a couple of satellite phones which were blocked by the Israelis after night set in.

When dawn came and we hadn't yet been attacked, we knew we had survived the dark but were still braced for Israel's probable attack. After all, they had told us bluntly that we would not be allowed to sail to Gaza. Many hours later, we were elated to see on the dusty horizon, the shores of Gaza. We started to believe we might actually make it all the way.

At about 15:30, we heard through the one functioning satellite phone that the Israeli military had decided not to stop us. At the 20-mile offshore marker, the place where Israel had threatened to board and harm us, our two boats were the only ones in sight. We sounded our horns, gave a rousing cheer to all and headed for shore.

Most memorable for all of us on board were the little boats that suddenly appeared all around us about two miles offshore. These boats were filled with cheering men and boys waving flags; the boys jumping in the water to collect the "Free Palestine" balloons we dropped over the sides, then clambering onto the decks of our boats until we feared we would sink. To see 40,000 Palestinians waiting on the dock to greet us was a sight none of us will forget. They were trying to believe what they were seeing, what they hadn't seen in over four decades. The people of Gaza had been largely ignored for years, and they hoped for a sign the world might begin to recognize their plight.

We represented that sign. That first voyage in 2008 achieved exactly what we hoped it would. We opened the door just a bit, proving it could be done. None of the later actions, by land or by sea, would have been possible or even attempted if we hadn't climbed into two ramshackle boats with nothing but our determination and our naiveté holding us together.

Our story of how we came together, raised the necessary money, and pulled off the successful voyage, despite the prying

10

eyes of Israel's intelligence service, the Mossad, is often riveting. More to the point, it makes you understand the importance of taking a stand when you see an injustice rather than becoming complicit through your silence.

Liberty and Free Gaza moored in Cyprus, waiting to take us to Gaza, August 20, 2008.

Foreword

Col. Ann Wright, 2012

You might not expect someone with my background (having served in eight presidential administrations, beginning with Lyndon Johnson and ending with George W. Bush), to be writing a foreword for a book critical of U.S. foreign policy; particularly policies that protect the State of Israel no matter what criminal acts it commits, including many that have been so extraordinarily uneven and harmful to the Palestinians.

In March 2003, after almost four decades of U.S. government service, I resigned from the U.S. State Department in opposition to the Iraq war.[1] I said I disagreed with the Bush Administration's lack of effort in resolving this conflict and its indifference toward using its influence to resurrect the peace process. I said that, "We must exert our considerable financial influence on the Israelis to get them to stop destroying cities and on the Palestinians to curb their youth suicide bombers."

Since my resignation over seven years ago, I have been using my voice from long U.S. government experience to attempt to end the wars on Iraq and Afghanistan, to stop U.S. sponsored torture, and to end unnecessary curtailment of civil liberties as a direct result of the Patriot Act.

It has been in the past four years that I have added my voice and presence to those who have been working so tirelessly to end unjust treatment of the Palestinian people by the United States and Israel.

It was the twenty-two-day Israeli assault on Gaza in December 2008 and January 2009 that jolted me into action. I went to Gaza for the first time in late January 2009, ten days after the brutal Israeli attack ended. As a twenty-nine-year U.S. Army veteran, I was stunned by the amount of destruction. The Israeli attack with American F-16 jets, drones, American

Apache attack helicopters, American white phosphorus bombs, and American dense inert metal explosive bombs killed 1,440 Palestinians including 380 children. The attack also wounded over 5,000 and left 50,000 homeless.

Entire areas had been systematically smashed with American–made weapons. Housing for over 50,000 had been blown up; people were living in tents and piled into family and friends' apartments that were very small and already crowded with their own immediate families. The electrical grid, and water and sewage systems had been destroyed. Schools and hospitals were severely damaged. Ambulances were destroyed. Ambulance crews risked their lives to take injured persons out of destroyed neighborhoods by wheelbarrow.

I decided to help groups get into Gaza and see for themselves the disproportionate force that the Israeli military used against the few people in Gaza who had sent homemade, unguided rockets into areas of Israel along the border with Gaza. In the next six months, I worked alongside many others with CODEPINK: Women for Peace. We were able to get hundreds of international activists into Gaza. These activists returned home to speak of the unbelievable destruction they witnessed there.

The stated objective of this blockade has been to strangle the Palestinians in Gaza until they overthrow Hamas, a political, militant, and social services group that won the most seats in the 2006 Palestinian Legislative Council elections. Hamas subsequently took over the governance of Gaza. Israel and the United States have put Hamas on their lists of "terrorist" organizations and are doing everything possible to make life so miserable for the people of Gaza that they "overthrow" the government. The blockade has resulted in the people of Gaza having to dig hundreds of tunnels underneath the border with Egypt to move food and supplies to keep people alive.

13

Other blockades have previously been used by the United States and other countries in an attempt to effect political change (i.e., overthrow of governments the United States does not like) in Cuba, Iraq, and Iran. But the result of these blockades is that the most vulnerable suffer: women, children, and the elderly. Seldom do the political leaders of the country suffer. None of the blockades have led to the change the blockading country intended. In contrast, citizen-initiated boycotts of goods from apartheid countries, such as South Africa, have been instrumental in effecting political change.

International citizen activists in the International Solidarity Movement (ISM) have protected Palestinian farmers, shepherds, and schoolchildren in the West Bank and Gaza. In the past three years, international citizen activists in five convoys of Viva Palestina have brought hundreds of vehicles and tons of medical supplies to Gaza following the twenty-two-day Israeli assault. In December 2009, the Gaza Freedom March brought 1,350 activists from fifty-five countries to Cairo in an attempt to march in solidarity with the people in Gaza.

But the Free Gaza movement is where a well-coordinated activist challenge to the illegal Israeli siege on Gaza all started. In August 2008, the Free Gaza movement began sailing small vessels into Gaza, directly confronting and bringing international attention to the naval blockade that isolated the port of Gaza from international trade for over forty years. This book is their collective story.

Over the next few months, another four voyages of the Free Gaza movement brought in internationals from around the world, including European Parliamentarians, to see for themselves the devastating results of Israel's policies in Gaza. The boats also brought in Palestinians to reunite with families they had not seen in decades and took out of Gaza Palestinians who needed medical treatment and students with international scholarships who were denied exit visas by the Israeli government. After the Israeli Navy rammed the *Dignity* in

14

December 2008 and almost capsized the *Spirit of Humanity* in January 2009, the Free Gaza movement decided on another strategy. The idea of sending not just one or two ships, but six or eight ships to challenge the Israeli blockade moved from concept to reality in May 2010 with Freedom Flotilla 1.

The unnecessary lethal force used by the Israeli Navy leading to the death of nine passengers on board the Mavi Marmara and wounding of more than fifty international activists, resulted in an international firestorm against the Israeli government. The pressure from activists on their governments not to let Israel "get away with murder" had some effect. The Israeli government modified the land blockade, allowing more types of goods and a symbolic increase in the volume of goods that could enter Gaza. However, two years later, it is still inadequate. The Israelis did not modify the naval blockade, ban on exports, or the travel restrictions on Palestinians in Gaza that have continued to make the Gaza Strip a large "open-air prison" for its people.

I was honored to be a participant on the 2010 Gaza Freedom Flotilla and to work with the tremendous Free Gaza movement team that pulled the flotilla together.

In the face of the Israeli criminal actions of murder, piracy on the high seas, detention, and abuse of hundreds of human rights activists, including theft of personal possessions during the May 2010 Gaza flotilla, we have only become more determined. Although Greece stopped Freedom Flotilla 2 from leaving last July as Israel outsourced the occupation to Greece, we continue to plan and work on new ways of challenging Israel's illegal blockade.

The steadfast commitment of the Free Gaza movement to challenging the Israeli blockade is one of the great historical nonviolent actions by citizen activists, and I am very proud to be a small part of it.

Chapter 1: You Will Never Make It

Greta Berlin

The sun was shining in Cyprus when *Free Gaza* and *Liberty* finally pulled out to sea at 9:00 am, and 44 passengers, journalists and crew had this overwhelming feeling of joy. We were finally sailing to Gaza. Crowds lined the dock and cheered us on as *Free Gaza* cast off her lines and headed out of the port, only to find that *Liberty* had engine trouble again. We had to wait for two hours as the engineer climbed down into the engine room and fixed the fan belt. Finally, the Cypriot Coast Guard escorted us to the 12-mile limit before sounding their horns and turning back. We were on our way, three weeks late, but finally leaving, sailing 240 miles across the Mediterranean to the imprisoned people of Gaza.

The Israeli government had been threatening us for weeks, demanding that we abort the mission, telling us they could not be responsible for our safety (as though we were somehow sailing to Israel and not to Gaza, a territory that Israel had been telling the world was no longer occupied.) We had found Israel's Achilles' heel, and we were exploiting it in the media.

Israel had said it no longer occupied Gaza and had not occupied since the government pulled out its illegal settlers in 2005. Therefore, by Israel's own admission, Gaza was free to invite anyone who wanted to come and visit, to sail into its port and be welcomed. We were not asking for Israel's permission. We didn't need to. Gaza was free, and we were coming.

Our two boats could only travel at 7 knots, so we were in for a long and treacherous voyage, 33 hours until we would arrive, the threats from the Israeli government and its supporters of sinking us, then letting us drown, ringing in our ears. The day before we left, my phone rang.

"Do you know how to swim?" said the muffled voice. "What?" "Do you know how to swim?" he repeated. "What?" Shouting into the phone. "DO YOU KNOW HOW TO SWIM?"

Off the top of my head, I said, "I'm sorry. I can't hear you. You sound as though you're under water." At the time, I thought my answer was pretty funny.

Our high-profile passengers like Lauren Booth, sister-in-law of Tony Blair, had been threatened constantly, one caller saying he knew where she lived in France, and she had better go home and watch over her children.

Those of us working with the media had our phone numbers posted on the website as contacts. We often got 'anonymous phone calls' in the middle of the night. "There is a bomb on board." "You will never make it." "We know how easy it is to sink you."

We had scuba divers checking the undersides of the boats four times a day, looking for sabotage. Even the Cypriot Coast Guard went under the boats while they were docked in Larnaca. They didn't trust the Israelis either after the bomb attack in Limassol in 1988, and many in the port authority had talked to us privately, telling us that Israeli agents had been down to the port asking questions. This afternoon, they had given us a thumbs-up and said we were ready to sail.

We knew the Israeli government was watching us. We knew they wanted to stop us. We also knew the story of the Ship of Return, due to set sail in February 1988 from Cyprus. It was carrying Palestinians and supporters who were sailing back to Haifa to return to their homeland. Israeli frogmen blew up the engine with a mine stuck under the vessel. It was attached to a time fuse, according to port officials in Limassol.[1]

The blast came less than 24 hours after a car bomb on the waterfront killed three senior Palestinian organizers who were involved in plans for the voyage. There was only one

17

possibility who killed them, and that was Israel. So we took their warnings seriously.

No boat full of internationals had docked in the port of Gaza for 41 years, as Israel tightened the screws of their 20 year illegal blockade ever tighter since 2000, a blockade they said was all about security, and we knew was about stealing the natural gas of Gaza. They just didn't realize their threats made passengers more determined than ever to sail. We had come on this journey from 17 countries, from Palestine to Pakistan, from the U.S. to Europe. Most of us were activists and had worked in the occupied West Bank and Gaza, some for decades. Threatening us was completely counter-productive.

So far, everything was working, as the boats sneezed and snorted their way across the waves, their diesel engines complaining. The two captains, John Klusmire from the U.S. and the Greek captain, Giorgos Klontzas, were talking to each other on Channel 16, used for transmissions by ships of the world. Their readings said we might be in for some rough weather but no rain, just choppy constant waves.

We watched Larnaca twinkle into the distance as a cheer went up from both boats, "We are coming." The journalists from Al Jazeera and Ramattan got on their satellite phones and called ahead to Gaza, "We Are Coming." It was to be the last set of phone calls made.

Within two hours, beam seas started rolling the two boats around like pieces of debris. Those of us on *Free Gaza* were doubly pitched from side to side, because the boat had a useless mast that tipped dangerously close to the water as Captain John tried to wrestle it upright. Almost all of us were sick, and the misery was made worse by the spray coming up and over the boat, drenching us and making the deck a slippery mess. We held onto the rails, some even crawled along the outside of the deck, as we tried to navigate to narrow benches set into the sides of the boat and lie down. The seasickness pills and patches were of little use, as our own fear of what might happen added to our sickness.

After ten hours at sea, the sun began to set, a filmy disk slipping into the water's edge. We had long lost sight of land and saw no boats. Sharyn Lock, a major organizer from Australia, announced that we were 70 miles away from Cyprus, and we all groaned. It was going to be a long night.

Thirty minutes after the pitch black descended on the two boats, our radio, mobile and satellite phones went dead. The Israeli navy had blocked all communications. We had made plans to keep one satellite phone off at all times, so they couldn't pick up the number, and we didn't dare turn that one on until there was an absolute emergency. Captain John said the Israeli communications system would pick up the number almost at once. The only means of communicating with each other was over the low-tech equipment we had brought on board; walkie-talkies. Jeff Halper, chairman of the Israeli Committee Against House Demolitions was on board our boat and told us we wouldn't see or hear the Israelis coming if they decided to attack.

One of the journalists was clutching his camera to his chest and lying on the deck of the boat, determined that, if anyone attacked us, he was going to get footage. My friend, Mary, was propped up in the Zodiac, the little rubber boat used for emergencies. She was throwing up in rubber gloves, tying them neatly at the top, and handing them to me to throw overboard. We had laughed at Kathy Sheetz, the emergency room nurse from California who was on board. She had insisted we buy biodegradable rubber gloves, never thinking they would be used for vomit.

"Here," Mary whispered, "Throw this one overboard and give me a new one." The glove bobbed off into the waves. "If the Israelis board, they'll have to lift me up or shoot me right here in the Zodiac, because I don't have the strength or will to follow their orders." I hoped that was not going to happen.

Even though it was August, it was cold on the water, and we had not prepared ourselves for the damp. The water had drenched everything and everyone. We had two options; stay above on the deck and be cold and wet, or go down below to the six cabins and inhale the diesel fuel. The cabins were dry, but the diesel fuel made even the experienced sailors gag. Most passengers chose to stay above.

At 22:00, a fire started in the engine room of the *Free Gaza*, and Derek was down in the hold covered in ash and soot, trying, with two volunteers, to put out the fire and keep the engine running.

I closed my eyes and thought of the two years it had taken us to buy and board these boats and head out to Gaza. People thought we were insane, and, at the moment, I was beginning to believe they were right. The entire journey had been organized through the Internet, and every passenger coming with us had been recommended by at least two other people. Our original passenger list of 88 had dwindled down to 44 as the voyage was postponed, then postponed again, then postponed again. Everything from the suicide of one of the organizers to running out of money had delayed the trip.

Many of us were veterans, working in the occupied territories, but some, like Musheir El Farra, an engineer from the U.K., just wanted to go home to see his family. The Israeli government had refused to allow him to attend his mother's funeral, and he wanted to say his 'good-byes' to her. Coming with us was his opportunity to enter Gaza without the humiliating searches from Israeli soldiers that all Palestinians trying to enter or leave Gaza endured.

Since 2006, when we decided we would sail to Gaza, the five of us who had organized this voyage had split our responsibilities; Paul Larudee was in charge of the boats, I was in charge of the passengers, Mary Hughes Thompson was in charge of finances, and Renee Bowyer and Sharyn Lock were in charge of logistics. We had managed to grow from five dedicated people to over two hundred in two years, working together via Internet with the overriding goal of sailing to Gaza. I crawled into the other end of the Zodiac to try to get some sleep and decided to calm my own queasy stomach by making lists in my head. I ran over the checklists one more time.

Were all 44 passengers checked in and on board? Yes. The oldest was Sister Anne Montgomery, an 81-year-old nun from the U.S. who had worked in Palestine for the Christian Peacemaker Teams and had also worked in Iraq. The youngest, Adam Qvist, was a 22-year-old Danish activist from the International Solidarity Movement whom I had met in 2007 as he was walking Palestinian children to school in Hebron under the malevolent gaze of the illegal settlers.

Did everyone know how to swim? As far as we knew, they did and had signed the waiver saying they knew how (we found out later that several of our passengers could barely dog paddle in the children's end of the pool.)

Had everyone made out a will? Yes. We had no idea what was going to happen, and Ramzi Kysia, head of our land team in Cyprus, had insisted everyone write a will, then send or give one copy to family or friends and leave a copy with him. Some of the passengers thought we were being overly dramatic. It turned out, two years later when the Israelis murdered nine people on our Freedom Flotilla, that it was a good idea to have a will. We also had to leave a contact number, our passport numbers and country of issue and our wishes for getting rid of our bodies.

Almost everyone agreed to be buried at sea, although some wanted to be refrigerated and sent to Gaza, a lofty goal considering the refrigerator on board could only hold soft drinks.

Had we all signed a waiver absolving the Free Gaza (FG) movement of any liability? Yes. We would not have taken them otherwise. We had no money and no liability insurance. Every cent that we had raised went into the boats, more than $700,000 by the time we finally boarded them. These donations had come from all over the world, from people as outraged as we were that 1.5 million Palestinians were boarded up in an outdoor prison.

Did we all have life jackets and had we been at the safety session run by our irrepressible Irish first mate, Derek Graham? As far as I could tell in the pitch darkness, everyone on board the *Free Gaza* had on a life jacket.

I looked around the boat, seeing small orange humps on the deck and people leaning over the rails retching, attached to the 'throw-up lines.' We could see across to the *Liberty*, where three of their passengers, wearing orange, were also attached. Derek had reminded us that, under no circumstances were we to throw up without being connected to the line.

"I'm not coming to fetch ye," he yelled in an Irish accent. "If you're fucking stupid enough to throw up over the side and go over, you can fend fer yerself."

Later, he told us that would never have happened, but he knew we were unaware of how dangerous the waves really were, and if he had to scare the crap out of us, that was fine. Except for the ten members of the crew, five on each boat, none of us had any sailing experience, except on a lake.

I drifted off to a fitful sleep, counting rubber gloves, only to be shaken awake an hour later.

"We need volunteers in two-hour shifts. People who aren't sick, four to a shift, front and back." Derek demanded, and several of us on board volunteered to stand watch in two-hour shifts, not to look for Israeli gunboats, but to make sure our boats didn't collide with each other. The only way the crews on board could talk was via walkie-talkie, and they had to be pretty close, almost impossible in the tossing sea.

Seventy-nine year old David Schermerhorn, a film producer from the state of Washington with years of experience on boats, volunteered for the 1:00-3:00 am shift, along with me,

Sharyn, and Vittorio Arrigoni, a veteran of the sea and a long-time activist and journalist from Italy. I went back to sleep for two hours, rocking in the Zodiac that was attached to the deck. At 1:00 am, David woke me up.

"Time for us to stand watch. It's pretty quiet right now, most are asleep, but you'll have to be careful at the stern of the boat. One person back there is pretty sick." I wandered back to the stern and looked out to see if there was anything that could be seen. The stars were out, but, other than the light on the stern of *Liberty*, there was nothing on the sea. How did the captains even know what was out there? We didn't have a single electronic device to even tell us if a ship was approaching.

Suddenly, at 1:30 am, Captain John and Derek both got violently ill, incapable of piloting *Free Gaza*. John and Derek were experienced sailors; John had piloted all of his life on big research ships. Derek had spent a good deal of his time on the sea. Had someone poisoned them? Was someone on board working for the Israelis? That had always been one of our fears; that no matter how much screening of passengers, one could be bought off or blackmailed into doing the bidding of Israel. Was I getting completely paranoid? I held on to the stern, looking at the back lights of *Liberty* and wondered if Giorgos was sick.

John handed over the boat to David and Vik after some wrangling with one of the other crewmembers that he, and only he, could pilot the boat. The two boats did their best to stay together, Giorgos, who apparently was fine, stayed on the walkie-talkie. I stood watch along with Sharyn

As long as we could see the lights of the *Liberty*, we felt a bit safer. In a couple of hours, John and Derek were fine. We never knew why they got so sick.

During the dark, cold, wet, miserable and frightening night, huddled together, those of us awake tried to stay upbeat. The three toilets down below deck had stopped working. Derek

23

had yelled at us not to put toilet paper down them, but no one remembered.

The fan belt on the engine on the *Liberty* continued to split, and we could hear the boat coughing as it chugged along. They were, after all, old fishing boats equipped to carry 11 passengers each, and we had 25 on one boat, 19 on the other. We didn't want to face the possibility we might have two boats with no engines, one with no captain. The worst possible scenario would be drifting at sea, and have the Israeli navy finally rescue us, laughing at our stupidity.

As one of the organizers of this ship of fools, I began to despair. What had we done? Had we put 44 peoples' lives in danger for some stupid idea of sailing to Gaza? Was our two years of organizing, the death of one of our primary supporters and the massive debt we had incurred trying to get the boats ready… was all of that going to go into the drink?

A little after 3:00 am, David woke up Ayash Darraji, the Al Jazeera journalist.

"Does your sat phone work?" David asked. "I know we said we wouldn't take the risk, but we have a really ill passenger on board, our equipment is dead and someone needs to know where we are."

Ayash turned on his phone, actually got a tone and called his office. Although we couldn't have known it out there in the dark, Al Jazeera released the story of our lost boats, the Greeks demanded to know where their MP was, and Israel, backing off, stopped jamming our electronics. But it took two hours until the two satellite phones were working, and daylight before the navigating equipment was back online.

My shift was more than over, and I was exhausted. It was 4:00 am. That night was one of the longest nights in all our lives. As the dark slowly faded, we could see boat lights in the distance behind us and wondered if they were Israeli gunboats.

I curled up next to Mary in the Zodiac and thought about how it had all started.

Chapter 2: In Memory of Riad

Greta Berlin, Michael Shaik, Riad Hamad, Sharyn Lock, Paul Larudee, Mazin Qumsiyeh

Greta

"How was this idea hatched to sail boats to Gaza? Who came up with such a crazy idea? Where did you get the volunteers? What were you thinking? Are you nuts?"

The idea came from Michael Shaik, a long-time activist from Australia. After Israel invaded Lebanon in 2006, several of us had been tossing around different ideas about how to bring to the attention of the world that Israel, while attacking Lebanon, had imprisoned Gaza.

Michael wrote the following to us:

> Okay. I have been thinking about this for a long time but am aware that I'm better at ideas than practicalities, so I'll outline what I'd envisaged and let the rest of you do the sanity check. My plan was this:
>
> Charter a big boat to sail from New York. Make it clear that its purpose is to, 'Break the siege of Gaza' (that can be the slogan of the campaign). It is very important that the boat have a big send off, with speeches by important people that will get it as much publicity as possible
>
> The ship sails to Gaza but stops along the way to pick up supplies from supporters. This would obviously require liaison with the relevant solidarity groups at the places where it was stopping.
>
> I was thinking of an itinerary along the lines of New York-Havana-London-Casablanca-Barcelona-Marseilles-Rome-Istanbul-Alexandria-Gaza
>
> The idea would be to build up publicity as we go. If we could get someone like Desmond Tutu to go at least part of the way,

that would really help put pressure on other religious leaders to see us and give the boat their blessing.

The hardest part would obviously be the Alexandria-Gaza leg of the trip. I doubt that the Israeli Defense Force (IOF) would try to sink the boat or anything.

Like I said, it's only an idea, and I don't know how much it would cost to charter a boat. It's a hell of a lot more ambitious than an airport sit-in, but I've been doing solidarity work for Palestine for almost four years now, and the situation on the ground there keeps getting worse and worse. I realize that just about everyone else reading this would probably share my frustration. So my thinking was that maybe it's time to think big and try to capture people's imaginations to force the issue.

He sent that message in September 2006 to a group of us who had volunteered with the International Solidarity Movement in the occupied West Bank and could not get back in.

Mary Hughes Thompson and I looked at each other and said, 'Let's do it.'

And thus an idea was hatched, and the Free Gaza movement was born. Who would be crazy enough to join us, and who did we know? I called Paul Larudee in the Bay area to see if he was interested. He had just come back from bearing witness to the massacres in Lebanon. Mary, Paul and I decided to start a small GOOGLE group of interested people who might be crazy enough to think we could buy a boat.

It turned out that several other people in other areas of the world were thinking the same thing. When we began to publicize that we were going to sail to Gaza—granted a much smaller project than what Michael has envisioned; activists began to add their ideas, asked to join our group, and the beginnings of a long two-year project started to take shape.

If we had known it would take two years, 250+ people, thousands of donors, and eventually close to 700 thousand dollars to sail two dilapidated fishing boats from Greece to

Gaza, I'm not sure how many of us would have signed on to this crazy adventure.

But several of us did. We signed on, not having the vaguest idea of how hard it was going to be to even find boats, much less buy them and sail them 240 miles from Cyprus to Gaza.

The first thing we needed was a boat buyer. I had known Riad Hamad since we had marched against Bush's war in Crawford, Texas in 2003 and called him.

Riad was crazy in love with the project, saying he was leaving for Turkey to find a boat that day, even though he had not left the U.S. since 2001. He emailed Paul and me every day to report. He knew we should keep the location of the boat a secret, so he sent us photos of boats that were in every port except the one he was dealing with, telling us what he found. We didn't realize at the time that Riad was manic in his support for Palestine, sometimes spending days without sleeping and squeezing his volunteer work between teaching in Austin, Texas.

We also didn't realize that the FBI and the IRS had been watching him for a long time. By 2004, he had a history of writing to officials in DC demanding that they leave him and his family alone. Where many Arabs and Muslims hid after 9/11, fearing for their safety (and for good reason), Riad was out there thumbing his nose at the government, a brave soul considering the time. The following is a letter Riad wrote on July 2004 to Attorney General John Ashcroft: [1]

Ref: Harassment of my children, monitoring my friends and family, intrusion on my privacy and civil rights.

My neighbor came up to me few weeks ago and informed me that an agent from the Federal Bureau of Investigation called him again regarding some information about my activities and other personal matters. Mr. Frank R. specifically told me that the agent inquired about the kind of car that I drive since your agents cannot find any records of car ownership for me in Travis country or the state Texas.

Your agents should know the car that I drive, since it has more than 20 bumper stickers in support of the people of Palestine, against the occupation of Palestine, against the war in Iraq and one that states, "A village in Texas is missing its idiot," and I think he now lives on 1600 Pennsylvania Avenue in Washington, D.C.

If you cannot identify the car and for your convenience, I have written " I am an Arab, *Ana Arabi*" in large characters (In English and in Arabic) on the rear window even a visually impaired person can see, unless they are blind in the mind and the heart like you and the rest of the administration that you represent.

I keep 300 dollars out of my paycheck, fifty percent of the rest goes to my two children for their college education and the other fifty percent goes to families and children that I sponsor in Palestine. Now, you know that piece. Anything else you want to know. Oh yes, I forgot, my personal attire.

I own five shirts: One light pink shirt that I have had for over three years. (I use it often to show my feminine side because I know how much you and the rest of this administration hate gays), one dark pink shirt that I have had for over three years, one blue George W. dumb-ass look style shirt with a hole under the armpit, one puke green shirt ala Tom Ridge's face with a stained collar, a chicken-poop yellow shirt, ala Ashcroft's face to wear to work on sunny days. Also, I have six pairs of socks, all with holes in them so that it would not allow me to take off my shoes at doctor's offices or during romantic encounters.

Other personal belongings include a large Palestinian flag, a large Iraqi flag, a small Palestinian flag to hang from left side back window of the car that I drive and do not own, a small Iraqi flag to hang from the right back window of the car that I drive and do not own, a membership card in the Law Library of the State of Texas, a membership card in the Public Library in Austin, Texas, a membership card in the University of Texas System libraries, five pieces of paper indicating that I have completed the requirements for seven college degrees and a piece of paper indicating that I have completed a proficiency test in the Japanese language at a college level.

He was just what we needed in a boat buyer, someone who would take a chance on us and not be intimidated. In two days, he sent us back a proposal for a boat.

> Please find attached the proposal for the boat project and I will call you later to discuss it with you to explain some items before you send it out for financing. The fixed cost is about 450 000 U.S dollars, [of course, we forgot that we were going to have to buy and outfit the boat in Europe, and the exchange rate at that time was $1.30 to the euro, so we would have to raise 30% more than we expected] and the variable cost of staff, fuel, food etc. will depend on the number of "tourists" that we get. Let me know if you have any questions and SHUKRAN[1] for your work and support. Riad Hamad

Riad was thorough. His proposal was well thought out and complete.

> Here is my proposal for internationals to travel between Gaza and Cyprus by sea. The service will be for facilitating travel for Palestinians and foreigners and to support the fisherman of Gaza by providing international support and to accompany them during their fishing trips.
> Rationale: Gaza is a historical port city that serves the southern regions of Palestine and an access to Egypt by land. The port has been closed to the outside world since 1967 and the passenger service is at a stand still due to the Israel.
> Additionally, the fishing fleet of Gaza is sitting idle since the Israeli navy imposed a three-mile security zone to prevent the fisherman from venturing out to the sea. Fishermen are shot it, arrested and the boats are confiscated frequently at will without any legal authority under international law. Furthermore, Israel claims that Gaza is free and that the blockade is lifted but the facts on the grounds are to the contrary. Thousands of Palestinians who live in Gaza are unable to travel abroad by air

---

[1] "Thank you" in Arabic

or by sea due to the blockade and the fishermen are hungry and unable to do the work that their families did for centuries.

Strategy: The Free Gaza Boat Project will create an avenue for the people of Gaza to travel to Cyprus and other destinations. Israeli response to the boats when they arrive in the international waters will create a media interest in the event and encourage dialogue and forces the international media to debate the blockade of Gaza that violates international law. The passengers of the boats and the crews will act exclusively through non-violent means and the management of the company that operates the boat.

Expenses and infrastructure required:
One large boat with a capacity to hold 36-40 passengers
One captain certified to sail and operate in international waters
Two crewmembers, including one diesel engineer to operate, repair and maintain the boats
One manager to oversee the operation of the boats, tours between Gaza and Cyprus and possibly other destinations at a later stage.
Cost: One large boat: $225 000, capacity of up to 40 passengers
Operating expenses: Salaries: Captain: $2000 a month plus vacation and health benefits
Crew: 2 crewmembers including the diesel engineer per month; $3500++
Manager: $35,000 per year plus benefits
Estimated fuel cost: 150 gallons/ day at $500 a day
Annual cost, one round trip a week between Gaza and Cyprus: $52 000
Cost of fuel when idle: 10 gallons a day to maintain the boats and ensure proper mechanical maintenance on regular basis or $40
Insurance and taxes: $15 000 annually
Registration and incorporation fees: $15 000
Total operating expenses for one year: $270,000.00

Revenues: [We thought we were going to be able to charge passengers for going, not realizing that Free Gaza would have to be registered as a commercial enterprise, when we weren't even registered to collect money for the project. Ultimately, we counted on donations to raise the money for the trips.] $320,000.00

Passengers year one: 1000 passengers or 40 passengers a week
    Fare per passenger per day: $50
    Estimated length of trip and days on water: 4 days per passenger
    Estimated trips per year: 40 trips
  Total estimated revenue in year one: $320 000

We were so naïve, we actually thought we could set up a ferry service between Cyprus and Gaza, and Israel would ignore us, not fully understanding that, even in the fall of 2006, Israel was already making deals with other countries in the region to exploit gas reserves under the water, and the last thing they wanted was a boat full of passengers seeing their rigs in the Med and shouting, "Free, Free Gaza" at the tops of our lungs as we sailed into the tiny port.

By the end of 2006, we were busy raising money, designing a website, www.freegazamovement.org, filing for charity status in the U.S., and pulling others into the project.

In November 2006, several activists in the UK had joined us. Sharyn Lock had written that they were organizing a 'sit in' at the Ben Gurion airport. When we asked if they would be more interested in sailing a boat to Gaza, she was ecstatic. Renee Bowyer, who had also been to the occupied West Bank and Lebanon as well, soon joined us. Our small working group was now growing to the six major organizers who would see the project through to the day we sailed: Mary, Paul, Renee, Sharyn, Riad (in memoriam) and me. We were joined by people from around the world who had the same goal we did; breaking Israel's illegal siege on Gaza.

We had one thing in common, even though we hadn't all met each other. We were all veterans of the International Solidarity Movement (ISM). Most of us had volunteered in either the occupied West Bank or Gaza since the movement began in 2002; many of us had been wounded, beaten, shot and tear gassed. All of us were pissed. We were super glued together by the common denominator of working with the Palestinians, and held together by our outrage over what Israel was continuing to do to the people it occupied.

In the early part of 2007, with Riad's proposal in hand, Paul, Mary and I decided to put together a fund raising 'tour of California' and start raising the money. Riad promised us that he would contribute $25,000 of money he would raise. Since I traveled to Texas to work with the oil business, I could work during the day, and then speak at night in Houston, Austin and Dallas.

My oil biz clients would probably not be happy with my extra-curricular work, but they didn't need to know either. After 5 pm, my time was my own. (That turned out to be true, until the 2010 Freedom Flotilla left for Gaza and Israel massacred nine of our passengers. As one of the spokesperson for the flotilla, I was extensively interviewed in the United States. When I returned in the fall of 2010 to start work again, every one of my clients dropped my services and I was forced to close my business.)

In June 2007, Mary, Paul, Riad and I all flew to the American-Arab Anti-Discrimination Committee National Convention in Washington, DC to beg for a few minutes of their time, so we could announce our mission to Gaza. They looked at us as though we were nuts, telling us that there was no time in the agenda for something as ridiculous as sailing boats to Gaza. Finally after much cajoling, they granted us 10 minutes at the end of the session on Palestine. At the end of ten minutes after a rousing speech, people were again handing us money out of their pockets and purses. We had come up with an idea that was different and exciting. Even if they didn't believe we would make it, they believed we thought we would make it. Several said they were sure they could raise money for us, but only Riad proved to be a man of his word and actually collected funds for the boat. It was hard to say 'no' to him.

As Paul and I were talking to the 40+ people in the room, Riad was out in the hallway, buttonholing every delegate he could talk to. He had driven a huge truck from Austin to Washington loaded with Palestinian goods. He was so sure he could set up and sell the goods that he never asked. He had printed in bright red and white 500,000 FREE PALESTINE, END THE OCCUPATION bumper stickers and had brought thousands of olive wood and mother-of-pearl pins to sell.

Of course, the DC police made it clear that he was not going to set up and sell anything from anywhere in any vehicle as long as they were patrolling the city. So Riad stood outside in the sunshine, handing out the buttons, banners, bumper stickers and jewelry for free. He never considered how he was going to pay for what he had brought. Ironically, he raised more money (as people handed him 'donations' for the boat) than if he had set up a tent.

When we met that afternoon, Riad was late. Mary, Paul and I were busy counting the money we'd raised, somewhere around $2000, when Riad came bounding in, his pink shirt soaked through, pulling money out of his pockets in little crumpled balls and throwing change on the floor to be counted; he had raised more than the $2000 we had just collected standing in the cool comfort of a conference room.

When he drove back to Austin, the huge moving van was almost empty, and, as he drove from town to town, he continued to empty it and collect donations. He said all he really needed to make a bigger impact was to buy a camel. To the day he died, he was trying to buy one.

It would be another 9 months before the U.S. government hounded Riad to his death.

After spending twelve months raising money, we had accumulated almost $50,000 in the US and close to $40,000 in the UK, enough for a down payment on a boat. We raised that

33

money speaking at any venue we could. At one in the UK in the winter of 2007, I announced that we were buying a boat and sailing it to Gaza, and people started throwing pounds at me. If I had been younger, I would have considered dancing on a pole to raise the money.

Riad had sent us more than $10,000 of his own money and was busy looking for boats in the Mediterranean.

At the beginning of 2008, we realized we would have to abandon our dream of buying a ferryboat and opening up a channel from Cyprus. We were beginning to realize we knew nothing about sailing boats. Even Riad knew nothing except how to find one. And we were getting concerned that we would not have the money we needed, even if we downsized. We wanted to sail in May 2008, and would have only six more months to raise what we then thought would be another $200,000+ to add to our $90,000.

Riad went into full-blown Riad mode, sending out appeals, writing to his friends in the Arab world. Little by little, our money grew with contributions as small as $1.00 to as large as $20,000. We were well on our way to raising the $300,000 we thought we'd need.

By February 2008, Riad had found the perfect boat and needed $50,000 to hold it. At the end of February, we transferred $25,000 to Riad to make a down payment on a boat. He was going to match the amount. We were ready to purchase. And then, on February 28, 2008, this message came to Paul, Mary and me:

Marharba[2], I just tried to log in and the system would not let me in. called the bank and they have an order to close my accounts...heads up and take the necessary steps...will call you tonight as I have an appointment with an attorney about my job...which is in jeopardy now...oh, well. I hope some

---

[2] "Hello" in Arabic

Palestinians are willing to pay the price that I am paying now...as I go with my fight alone...or so it seems. More later, and SHUKRAN for your work and support. Salamat[3], Riad Hamad

The FBI had raided Riad's apartment, taking everything they could, the IRS had frozen his accounts; but what had devastated Riad the most is that they went after his children. A week later as Paul and I were trying to set up a defense account for Riad, we got this email from him:

> March 7, 2008 Please note date and time of email and the next day the ATT men were outside for two days...and then ONE dark looking man carried the FedEx and boat project documents in his own hands separate from the rest of the computers, boxes...etc...all a cover up...NO MORE phones please and emails ONLY for fundraising for legal defense for ALL of us... SHUKRAN for your work and support, Salamat, Riad Hamad

We sent $500 as quickly as we could to help Riad in court and we talked to an attorney who said that he was over-reacting, but Riad was inconsolable. They had come after his children.

> March, 13, 2008 I put my life and the safety of my children and what did I get ... Also, even if you have $100, 000 today, with the political turmoil in the region NO ONE will sell a boat on loan...my life is ruined, and I might lose my job next week when I go back to work. And that means, not even money to make payments for myself...getting racist phone calls at home again...from students and others...I have no illusions. I am very realistic and have been all my life...please consider being up front with the group about the status of the boat purchase and consider going on to another project to utilize your passion, energy and great minds BUT who am I to tell anyone...my regrets for anything that I might have said or

---

[3] "Hello" or "Goodbye" in Arabic. Literally, "peace be with you."

done to harm you, the group...including my children Shukran for your work and support for the children of Palestine. Salamat, Riad Hamad

Now Riad would only talk to us by phone, not willing to put anything into writing for fear it would hurt his children. Paul and I could not get through to him that everything would be OK, and we had set up a list serve to raise money for him and had sent out the notice to everyone about what the U.S. government had done. He called us three and four times a day in desperation that his daughter would lose her rights to become a doctor and his son would be kicked out of college. He stopped taking his medication, and he started to turn over some of his accounts to us. We should have known, but we didn't. We had always known Riad as the happy-go-lucky fixer of all things. We had only seen him in his manic phase. One month later, Riad committed suicide.

On April 16, 2008, according to the media, the Austin Police Department determined Riad's death was a 'suicide,' despite his body being discovered gagged and bound with duct tape.[2] The Austin papers stated:

Last February, while Riad Hamad was readying himself for another school day, the technology instructor's small Austin, Texas apartment was raided by more than a dozen FBI agents and police. The police were searching for something to implicate the founder of the Palestinian Children's Welfare Fund in: "wire fraud, bank fraud, and money laundering."

He was also very outspoken about international politics, objecting strongly to Israeli and U.S. policy in the Middle East. Partly as a consequence, he had been investigated by federal authorities, who asked questions of some of his neighbors, and in February, the FBI and Internal Revenue Service raided his South Austin home and seized 40 boxes of materials related to his charity work, reportedly pursuant to an investigation of alleged "wire fraud, bank fraud, and money laundering." Although no charges had been brought, the raid greatly disrupted Hamad's charity work.[3]

No federal indictment had been issued against Riad, but according to Sgt. Greg Moss, APD missing persons investigator, Hamad's wife mentioned the FBI investigation as having placed great emotional stress on him and as a reason for being particularly concerned when he went missing – that he might be tempted "to do harm to himself."[4]

We had lost our friend, a man who lit up a room when he walked in, a man who was often more pro-Palestinian than the Palestinians. And Riad took the boat information to his watery grave. There will always be speculation whether he killed himself or Mossad killed him, but those of us who knew him well, knew that the U.S. government killed him...just not directly. We were left with no boat and $25,000 of our money gone and never returned. And we said we were leaving in May.

Sailing for Riad

Sharyn Lock

Riad was our boat buyer and passionately supportive of the plan to sail to Gaza. At the time he was raided, he was about two weeks away from buying our first boat using $50,000 of our money and his money as a down payment. None of his contacts were safe after that and the information about the boat was permanently lost.

He'd been aware of low-key FBI surveillance for a long time; he was used to it and made a joke of it. But he'd never been raided, and the results of the raid sent Riad over the edge. He also sold Palestinian products on behalf of many people there, but he'd never gotten one step ahead of himself financially, in terms of being able to pay his suppliers in advance of sale.

So, they sent him the goods, he sold them, and sent the money back. Well, now he couldn't send the current money owed because the account was blocked. This was extremely distressing for him; he hadn't enough money of his own to cover it.

Of course, this could have been worked out somehow, but then it was coupled with the FBI questioning both his son and daughter, causing the family great stress. This was just too much for Riad. I think he felt himself to be a risk and a trouble to the family and Palestinian projects he loved.

He handed personal details and project information over to close friends, drove his car to his local lake and waded into the water. His hands and feet were taped together, but despite the inevitable speculation, people close to him believe this was suicide; perhaps he was ensuring he would be successful, making a point about being forced into this choice.

Was the FBI raid based on a timely Israeli tip meant as an obstruction to our efforts? If so, we lost much more than a boat. I read the many eulogies from his memorial service; he was doing an impossible number of things for an impossible number of people.

For example, while we were in Lebanon, my friend, Renee was asked by Riad to visit a Palestinian family with two severely disabled children. She wanted to buy them wheelchairs and beds that wouldn't come to them in any other way. And Riad got them both wheelchairs and beds. He took other people's suffering as something he should personally address.

It was now the end of April, and we had promised people we were sailing in the summer, and we had no boats. That's where the Greeks came in; a contact from one of our activists brought them into the project.

So we are also sailing for Riad. His e-mails are still in my inbox; I can't bring myself to delete them.

My colleague Paul was probably the last to speak to him.

Paul Larudee: Riad's Last Phone Call

It was April 15, 2008. "Hi, Riad." I knew it was him from the caller ID, even though the phone had never been in his own name.

> "Hey, Bolous. How you doin'?" He used the Arabic translation of my name. "I'm good. How about you?"

> "I'm okay." His voice didn't have the usual energy, but perhaps he was in a place where he couldn't speak loudly. "I sent you a couple of e-mail messages." "Yes, I saw them." The messages were about helping with his charitable work on behalf of Palestinians. There were a few things I didn't understand about the messages, so Riad cleared them up for me. "Now it makes sense," I said.

> "Okay. Well, that's all I wanted to tell you."

Typical Riad—always in a hurry to get off the phone.

> "Wait, I've got some good news!" "Oh, yeah? What is it?" He sounded surprised. "We're finally getting donations here. A check for a thousand came in today."

> "That's nice. Well, gotta go."

> "Oh, Okay. Take care of yourself."

> "You, too, Boulos."

Those were apparently Riad's last words, spoken from his car near Ladybird Lake in Austin, Texas. At the time I had thought it slightly odd that Riad was repeating what he had already told me by e-mail. I think he just wanted to hear a familiar voice. The police found the phone and car keys on the seat of the

39

unlocked car, typical of Riad to think of the person who would find the car.

I wish I had told him that the person who sent the check had also written a letter thanking him for the gifts of handmade Palestinian crafts and other items that Riad had sent as a thank you for a previous donation. He had also included handmade thank-you cards from his two young daughters. The older daughter, age eleven, had written, "Live in peace on the world. Everybody should LOVE! I am sad because people should be nice to you, but they are not."

The younger, age eight, had written, "I hope you start to live in peace." I would have read them to him over the phone if he hadn't been so anxious to end the conversation, but I decided to send them to read later and enjoy the children's drawings. The father's letter was longer and more specific in his praise for Riad's tireless efforts on behalf of Palestinians and their rights.

> I have included two checks for the needs of Palestinian children. It is my hope that you will use it to create hope for those oppressed. As we both see the dollar's value sink, the value of life especially in the eyes of the Creator never loses value. I extend this help to you and these children as if they were my own. We have the misfortune in living in very dark times, but in that darkness hope, love, and peace shine like the sun. To those that plant hope, they shall harvest peace.

Harvest peace, Riad. SHUKRAN for your work and support. Salamat.

Mazin Qumsiyeh: Riad's memorial, May 10

In the past few hours I kept contemplating what to say here. You can see from this sheet that my original talk here is all marked off, edited and changed and will likely be rambling. But I did hope I could preserve a few important things I wanted to say and add others, but that has been difficult. Several things cross my mind rather quickly the first few seconds of meeting Riad over 8 years ago.

He talks too much! He is too good to be true, and then (and this was mentioned by other speakers) I would like to know more about this guy. The parking lot outside the Church has several cars with bumper stickers, "Free Palestine". Those are the stickers Riad made and for which I recall that the last time we talked, he asked me if I have received the new batch that he sent me through a mutual friend. Like others here and as always, when people leave us, we always wish we had said a few more things to them. We wish we had told them more how we appreciated them.

So here goes. Riad was always on the run. When he did sit for a while like he did when he stayed at our home in Connecticut, the conversations were always very interesting. They ranged from weighty matters like the future of the Arab world to the mundane (like why I am failing at growing the Palestinian faqoos plant in my garden when I could grow everything else). The famous Lebanese American poet Khalil Gibran once said, "You give very little when you give of your belongings, it is when you give of yourself that you truly give."

Khalil and Riad will be remembered for giving of themselves. When I first met Riad before he started the Palestine Children's Welfare Fund, he was most passionate about the deteriorating situation of Palestinians living under occupation and in refugee camps. In life, there are those who are doers and those who are talkers, and Riad was definitely a doer so it did not take him long to figure out where he could personally contribute. His love of children was not just because 60% of Palestinians are under the age of 18. Every other sentence he uttered you would hear from Riad seemed to contain things like "for the Children", how about the children?

Already, the year before he founded PCWF, Israeli occupation forces killed over 200 Palestinian children and

41

hundreds were injured. But the impact on those not injured or killed was also devastating, with unemployment reaching 60%, more than twice what it was at the height of the Great Depression in the US. Riad's solution was direct aid by selling Palestinian products, by collecting donations and funneling money to those in need.

Some of us have thought he was going too fast and thus putting himself and his projects at risk. But Riad's impatience was in the context of a relentless war carried out by Israel with the support of the US against the people of Palestine. Riad always spoke fast and passionately that sometimes it was hard to keep up with him; but I think his mind was running even faster, always thinking of new ways to do things. They were always practical things.

As an example, when Riad read of my father's death, he took initiative to ask that a tree be planted in my father's honor and he sent me a picture of it. That picture had more value than any words of condolence he could have sent. That was the Riad we knew, always thinking practical things, not mere words. Reverend Martin Luther King, Jr. stated: "Cowardice asks the question, 'Is it safe?' Expediency asks the question 'Is it politic?' Vanity asks the question 'Is it popular? But conscience asks the question 'Is it right?'"

And there comes a time when one must take a position that is neither safe, nor politic, nor popular. But one must take it, because it is right. We know Riad followed his conscience and acted because it is right, not safe; and as Ralph Waldo Emerson summed it up well in his poem:

> What is success?
> To laugh often and much;
> To win the respect of intelligent people and the affection
>   of children;
> To earn the appreciation of honest critics and endure the
>   betrayal of false friends;

To appreciate beauty; to find the best in others;
To leave the world a bit better, whether by a healthy child,
    a garden patch or redeemed social condition;
To know even one life breathed easier because you have
    lived;
This is to have succeeded.

I think Riad succeeded beyond even his own imagination. I think most of us humans are generally more afraid, not that we are capable of changing things, but afraid that we are capable beyond our imaginations. I think we have to learn to appreciate ourselves, and the people around us, more.

To Riad's wife, Diana, his children, his family, thank you for giving us Riad/sharing him with us and with Palestine. We know Riad would want us to take care for each other and to say thank you to those who give of themselves. We know he would want us to intensify our work to help the oppressed. We know he cared about Palestine and recognized the centrality of its struggle for freedom. To continue Riad's work is thus the right thing to do.

Rest in peace my friend Riad. We will continue your work..."for the Children".

When we finally sailed in August 2008, many of us boarded the two fishing boats dressed in pink as a tribute to Riad. We had hundreds of "Free Palestine, End the Occupation" bumper stickers stored away in the hold of the boat. We were, indeed, sailing for Riad as much as sailing to break Israel's illegal siege on Gaza.

Riad, in the light shirt (pink of course) in 2007, handing out his Palestinian pins to everyone who he could talk to about the boats to Gaza.

Chapter 3: All Aboard the Free Gaza Movement

Mary Hughes Thompson, Hillary Smith, MP Jamal El-Khoudary, Greta Berlin, Vangelis Pissias, Petros Giotis, Bill Dienst

It was now May 2008, we were $50,000 in arrears; our boat buyer was gone and we had already announced we were going in May. So, we put out a call to our lists after Riad's death and said we were sailing in his memory. And we hoped to go by the end of July from Cyprus. Donations began to come in faster than we ever expected - a tribute to Riad's life. Within a few days, the $50,000 we had lost to the FBI had been replaced, plus more and we were looking for a boat buyer.

Mary Hughes Thompson

When we sent out a plea for donations, thousands of people contributed; some big, but mostly, they were small donations; $1.30 coming from Indonesia, for example. These donors were strangers; they believed in what we were trying to do enough to help us. I wrote and thanked every one of them, and many wrote back to say they were honored to contribute, that we were actually doing something brave. Many donated more than once; people wrote to say they were on a fixed income and wished it could be more. One woman sent us her social security check...twice. We had USS *Liberty* survivors donating every month from their Navy pensions. Looking back over what most would have considered overwhelming odds against us, I'm still humbled at the faith so many people had in our efforts from the beginning, when it seemed we had an insurmountable mountain to climb to raise the money.

The Free Gaza movement was on the cusp of the Internet/Social network phenomena. When we organized the first trip in 2006, TWITTER wasn't even around and didn't really start until mid-2007; Facebook was only two years old, not yet a public phenomenon and YouTube was only a year old. The remainder of the social networks didn't exist at all.

Therefore, we organized everything through GOOGLE groups, just trusting each other that our goal of sailing to Gaza would overcome our personal peculiarities. For the most part, that held through the entire planning stage. Social media got its tryout with Free Gaza, and we succeeded in making the project work without ever having met most of the organizers. We did have one thing in common. All of us had been volunteers with the International Solidarity Movement, so we trusted each other.

As social media becomes the major tool to organize and plan events from the Arab Spring to the Occupy Wall Street movement, we can be proud that Free Gaza was a pioneer in its use. The world will never be the same again. All of the initiatives since our first trip, from Viva Palestina to the convoys to Gaza, were a result of our success with Internet organizing.

Hillary Smith, a UK Volunteer

We activists in the UK were working like crazy to raise our share of the money. My introduction into the world of the Free Gaza movement came at a public meeting in Sheffield in 2007, where, in spite of ourselves, we became entranced by this crazy idea being presented to us through the ubiquitous PowerPoint presentation.

But this was unlike any other PowerPoint presentation I had seen. It thrilled us. However, we are a pretty sensible bunch of activists, and we thought we knew a thing or two about fund-raising for a cause as "controversial" as the

46

Palestinians. So we asked the tough questions: How much is this going to cost? On hearing that it would be a modest (!) $300,000, we protested that it didn't sound anywhere near enough (as if we knew anything about boat buying or sailing across the Mediterranean). And then the killer question—how much have you raised so far? Oh...well....

So it was a great idea—but was it ever going to happen? I'd had a bit of experience getting funding from trusts for relatively "unpopular" causes, and this felt like a challenge I couldn't resist. Like most people though, I was already involved in far too many things...and I still thought it wasn't really realistic.

And then Musheir El Farra, said, "Well, I need to be on that boat!" Musheir, who has lived in Sheffield for many years, is from Gaza and rages silently and not so silently about the way he is forbidden from traveling to his homeland. He is also the inspirational chair of Sheffield Palestine Solidarity Campaign and one of the reasons for my involvement in working with Palestinian people. Well, if he was on board, then I had to be on board too.

Sharyn and I spent many hours trawling through databases looking for likely trusts to which we could apply, and along the way we had some fairly tortuous phone calls. Try concisely answering the following: What are the aims of your organization? How are you going to achieve your aims? What are your short-and-long-term expected outcomes? The one I liked best was: Who are the likely beneficiaries of your project? If possible, give an estimate of the numbers."

Well, let's see—would one and a half million Palestinians, plus about two million of their relatives throughout the world, be enough for you?

And then, little by little, we got some money! Our first successful grant application was for £5,000 ($10,000 at 2008 exchange rate) and even better, when we converted it to dollars to let our friends across the Atlantic know, it sounded a lot bigger.

But the long slog of fund-raising was not particularly glamorous, and the number of trusts to which we could apply was pitifully small. Let's face it—most organizations are not interested in ideas about funding small boats sailing across the Mediterranean with the likelihood that they will be stopped and confiscated by the Israeli Navy. Added to that, was the challenge of working with a steering group based in the United States. They didn't seem to understand our need for financial information to make our applications seem even remotely sane.

After all, we were putting in applications for such an off-the-wall idea. The application itself had to come across as 100 percent boringly sensible and thorough. Part of the challenge, of course, was coming to terms with the well-known fact that British English and American English aren't exactly the same language. And while I was fussing, in my terribly British way, about the need for copies of constitutions and accounts, our colleagues in the States were coping with anxieties about so-called antiterrorism legislation.

In the end, we raised several thousand pounds from a few trusts, mostly trusts started by good old lefty families with a bit of cash and a conscience. My favorite was the £1,000 we were awarded by the Lipmann Miliband Trust, a fund in the name of socialist intellectual Ralph Miliband. I wonder what his son, the current foreign secretary of the British government, would feel about his father's legacy being spent on the boats that were going to break the siege of Gaza. This was the first of two interesting links between the Free Gaza movement and British politicians.

Calderdale and Manchester Palestine solidarity people put on fund-raiser after fund-raiser, overwhelming Sharyn (whose home region it was) with their enthusiastic work for a plan they could only support from a distance, and a diversity of groups and individuals all over the United Kingdom quietly handed over sums of various sizes.

View from the UK: A Backroom Perspective

As the plans for the boat departure began to seem more and more real, a little bit of e-mail discussion began to take place on how those of us left in Britain, the "backroom team," were going to support those in Cyprus and on the boat. It was also becoming increasingly clear that the backroom team was not so much a team as, well, approximately two of us.

Sharyn was really the lynchpin to much of the planning activity, including publicity, fund-raising, and communication between activists in different countries, but she was heading off to Cyprus or wherever (none of us knew from where the boats would start and that was fine by me). What I didn't know, I couldn't tell Mossad. Likewise, Renee and Osama, both heavily involved, would be either on the boat or the land team, as would Jonny. Other people, who had made contributions in the early days of the project were, for one reason or another, no longer able to give us much time.

Then came the news of Riad's death, and we were devastated. The launch time was moved to July, which gave us more time to organize and raise money, but Free Gaza organizers still had to find a boat.

We tried to set up what we optimistically called the UK support team. We could see two roles for ourselves: first, working to generate publicity and secondly, supporting and campaigning on behalf of the boat crew/ passengers if/when they got stopped or arrested by the Israelis. Since most of us thought this was the likely scenario, much of our attention was focused on this work, including identifying the members of parliament for our UK passengers in order to be ready to bang down their doors if our boat got impounded or the passengers were thrown into an Israeli jail.

We decided to hold a press conference in London and with the help of the London-based Palestine Solidarity Campaign. Jonny (later to join the Cyprus land team) was able to get some "names" who agreed to speak on our behalf.

Getting a press pack together that would attract attention was tricky for all sorts of reasons: basic factual information (like who the passengers were!) kept changing, much of the information was being kept secret, some of our activists did not want any personal publicity, and crucially, we had no photos of anything—not even the boats.

The other problem we faced was that although prospective passengers for the boat had been asked to provide short bios of themselves plus photos, only a minority had done so. This was very frustrating for those of us who were to trying to interest the media.

Of course, in a sense we didn't really want the individuals on the boat to be the story. The endurance and bravery of Palestinians in Gaza was the real story. The passengers didn't see themselves as heroes—but the dilemma was that we needed to make them famous in order to get the publicity that the boats needed in order to shout to the world that Gaza was under siege.

And then…I got a phone call. We had sent out an initial press release alerting media two weeks in advance about our planned press conference, which in turn was to be held about four days in advance of the departure of the boats. The day after the press release went out, the voice at the other end of my mobile said:

"Hello, I'm Lauren Booth, and I want to be on the boat." Pause…

I sort of felt as though I should know this person, but I didn't and I made that classic mistake of not saying so straightaway. As the conversation progressed it became clear that she was a journalist and that she was keen—no, not keen, absolutely 110 percent determined to be on our boat to Gaza.

I tried to explain that I thought that the first boat was full, that we had a list of interested people for the second boat, and that, although we were very keen to have some journalists on board, we needed a balance of people with different things to offer.

"Look," she said, in a polite but determined voice. "If I'm on that boat, and I get to Gaza two weeks after Tony Blair didn't, then it's going to be front-page news."

At last, the penny dropped: Blair...Booth...Blair—Booth! I ran upstairs to my computer, to see an e-mail from the Palestine Solidarity Committee office alerting to me to the fact that a journalist was about to phone me and that she was the sister–in–law of Tony Blair, former British prime minister. Blair was now the Middle East envoy for the Quartet. He had been in post for over a year and so far had not set foot inside the Gaza Strip. Blair was apparently oblivious to the conditions under which people were living there. Just two weeks previously he had canceled his first proposed visit to Gaza following "security advice" from Israel.

A flurry of e-mails to and from the States and elsewhere followed. Were we or were we not interested in having the sister-in-law of Tony Blair on board? Some rapid Googling revealed that Lauren had written some excellent articles about her previous visits to occupied Palestine (good) and that she had also been a contestant on the British reality TV show "I'm a Celebrity: Get Me out of Here" (bad—at least in the eyes of some of us more earnest activists).

There was some anxiety about involving a journalist who wrote pieces for British tabloids, but we were aware that Lauren was, of course, dead right. Her involvement would be a huge publicity coup for Free Gaza and not just in the UK but in the States and across the Arab world.

Independent MP Jamal El-Khoudary, Gaza

By the spring of 2008, the situation in Gaza was getting worse day by day. Even though Hamas had signed a 'Hudna' or temporary 6-month truce with Israel in June, Israel refused to open its blockade on our people. In fact, the Israeli occupation forces were closing the crossings and imposing a serious blockade on the Gaza Strip, making Gaza the largest prison in the world.

Therefore, a group of professionals in Gaza established the Popular Committee Against Siege (PCAS) to play a role in alleviating the effects of this blockade, and to reflect the agony of what was happening in Gaza to the whole world. When we started to look for partners to help get our message out, we received a prompt response from these heroes and peace activists of the Free Gaza movement who had been working hard to break through this blockade since the fall of 2006. They decided to defy the blockade and break it via two boats, *Liberty* and *Free Gaza*. They also decided to challenge the Israeli occupation, so that the Palestinian people in the Gaza Strip could live in dignity. We did not need handouts from the world. We needed our freedom.

We, ones who expected the success of this trip, were very few: only a handful of dedicated activists. In the late spring of 2008, we started to work hard with the *Free Gaza* Movement for the success of this creative and important work.

Our work was round-the-clock, but the most difficult task was that of the activists, whether in processing the ships, or the work of all necessary precautions for the success of the journey. With the help of the media, we started to exert huge and supportive efforts for the sake of the mission.

Finding the *Dimitris K* (the future *Free Gaza*)
Greta

April, 2008. I had a friend in Athens whose name was Georgia, and when we had no boat left and no prospect of a boat, she was one of the ones we wrote to, begging her to find us a Greek boat buyer. Surely, the Greeks, the maritime experts, the Poseidons of the sea, the authors of the Odyssey, would know someone who could buy us a boat. They must know someone. We had finally recovered our money and now had over $150,000 as a down payment to buy a boat, and we had a deadline of July staring us in the face, plus a lot of skeptics who were sure we would never go.

Georgia wrote to us that she had found the perfect person and he knew everything about boats. A week later, Paul and I got the following email from our new best friend, the boat buyer.

Vangelis Pissias in Athens, May, 2008

> Dear Paul, Greta, dear all,
> We can celebrate. We are serious. Just now I came back home from a shipyard a little bit far from Athens...I found it, an excellent boat, wood beams of high quality.
> Date of "birth" 1980: almost completely rehabilitated.
> A very close friend who I'd asked to make investigations in that area knows the story of this strong and safe boat. He was involved in rehabilitation work, and he assures follow-up for some marginal adaptations. He knows some local coastal authority administrators, so arrangements for legal possession and embarquement procedures will be easier in that region.

Vangelis is standing on board the newly purchased Free Gaza. Note there is nothing ON the boat except for Vangelis

The owner asked €150,000. We told him no more than €105,000 (if also engaged to install a new, same type, motor). He agreed after many hours of negotiation. No need for significant additional expenses, only some accessories and "comfort" equipment. I consider the price unexpected for that kind of boat, and I hope that with some more effort we can afford it. Perhaps we can make an additional effort for collecting some more money in Greece.

Length 21 meters (67 feet long)

Width 6 meters (21 feet wide)

Motor 365 hp, 1700 rpm, type: Penta Volvo, velocity 9-10 knots,

Fuel tank 4 cubic meter, strong high mast assuring efficient sailing, 8 cabins, 4 water closets Possible embarquement of 25 persons

Departure: +/- one month—maybe 45 days from the starting day of the final stage (including adaptation works and legal procedures) embarkation is possible.

Second boat carrying people not needed, just a small accompanying one (less than 6 meter length), very low price, only for carrying reserves and "safety reasons."

We were thrilled. A boat had been found and a picture sent to us with Vangelis standing on the deck. And it was $75,000 less than we thought we would need, even with the exchange rate. What we didn't know, because we were clueless, is that the boat came with nothing on it, not even a wheelhouse, and Vangelis didn't know any better than we did what was needed. He could find a boat, but he would have to count on someone else to tell us what we had to have on board.

Eventually our €105,000 ($135,000.00) investment ballooned to three times that amount. But we were so ecstatic; we said "yes, buy it." We didn't account for maintenance, crew, captain, fuel, food, mooring fees, activist lodging and general 'greasing of the palms' of several port authorities in Greece who looked the other way when the boats sailed. All in all, our $135,000 for the *Free Gaza* cost us $400,000+ just for her (not including the *Liberty*, another $250,000) by the time they limped into Larnaca, Cyprus, and we activists were paying for fuel on our credit cards, most maxed out to get the derelict boats into harbor.

Preparing the *Agios Nikolaos*, (Soon to become the *Liberty*) Petros Giotis: Notes of a Greek Journalist

It was in April of 2008 when Vangelis Pissias asked to meet with me. He told me about a project in which a group, consisting mainly of internationals, had been working for over a year and a half. The project was based on a simple idea: break the siege of Gaza by sea, since no one could access it by land

55

because of the blockade by Israeli and Egyptian authorities. Actually breaking the siege by sea would be a much more complex project.

The Free Gaza movement asked us Greeks to provide mission support: prepare a boat that could reach Gaza but prevent the Zionists spies from learning of the project and trying to sabotage our efforts. Until that time, prior attempts to purchase Free Gaza movement boats had failed. The Zionists had been able to get access to the boats on sale and managed to cancel their purchase. On the other hand, even if a boat could be purchased for FG, it always was at risk of being found and sunk by Zionists.

This means that an absolutely legal action (it is not illegal under international law to sail to Gaza) had to be accomplished in secret, as if it were illegal. So, for everyone's safety and for the success of the mission, we needed to conduct all our operations in the strictest secrecy every step of the way until and including mooring the two boats clandestinely in separate harbors around Athens. The whereabouts of one boat and crew would not be known to the other boat and crew. Each one of us involved in this project would function on a need-to-know basis, keeping the overall details as quiet as possible.

I didn't have to give it a lot of thought. I would join the mission at once. The Palestinian cause is a part of our collective conscience as Greeks. We grew up with it. We have always considered the Palestinian revolution our own cause.

We met Palestinian friends and comrades at university. We had helped them before with both open and clandestine activities. Thus, we couldn't say no. When it comes to helping the Palestinian people, who, for the last sixty plus years, have suffered under Israeli aggression and ethnic cleansing, I am completely on board. The Palestinians hold bravely the banner of the fight for freedom, and they are a beacon for all progressive peoples.

Vangelis took up coordinating this indispensable component of the Free Gaza mission's operations in Greece. Our friends from the FG abroad had already done an excellent job developing the political and financial support for this attempt. There was already an international group that represented seventeen countries that had requested to be on board.

Signatures had been collected in a petition gathering support for the attempt. There were already significant funds, but it was not sufficient. That would be the last of our concerns. We have learned that we must focus on what is most essential to get the job done. If we are to get anywhere with this mission, we must leave secondary matters like adequate financing aside. We must have faith that adequate funding will be dealt with when the time comes. (Easy for him to say, he wasn't raising the money, and the Greeks did not contribute money to this project. However, they were indispensable for finding, outfitting and moving the boats.)

The main aspect was the preparation of a boat that could take our multinational group to Gaza. As I have already mentioned, our mission had the unique challenge of having to be carried out in secret. If we went forth to the streets and announced that we wanted to buy a boat to break the blockade of Gaza, we would have found many supporters. The Greek people, no matter what their political affiliation, feel very close to the Palestinians. But this open public approach would probably have ended up with a sunken boat.

We had to act cautiously, involving a small number of people who wouldn't ask too many questions. Soon enough, Vangelis found the *Dimitris K.,* an old, but still good simple vessel that, with sufficient repairs, could be rendered seaworthy to carry some twenty-five people. This vessel would become the *Free Gaza.*

Then, a network of support was built that would ensure utter secrecy. People like Vangelis and I needed to keep a low profile, since the boat was already under repair in an area where Vangelis carried out research and many people knew him.

Nosy neighbors hanging around the marina would only learn that "the professor is building a boat to go on August holidays with his friends." That is not strange at all in a land like Greece with thousands of small or large private boats. Our network of people worked clandestinely, using methods devised during the fascist dictatorship in Greece (1967-1974). There was expertise as well as a positive social milieu: people have learned not to ask too many questions once they realize you are not willing to answer.

And those directly involved in a clandestine project are well aware that they should not be too curious; they knew only what they needed to know in order to accomplish their individual projects within the greater mission. Knowing much beyond the duties of their specific tasks could jeopardize the entire mission. Protecting the mission is of paramount importance. Thus, what is required is maximum secrecy and decentralization, that is, use of a network, most of whose member links are unaware of the other members' specific activities or whereabouts.

When the repairs on the *Dimitris K* (*Free Gaza*) had progressed enough, our friends abroad informed us that there were already a high number of participants and that we needed another boat. Time was running extremely short however.

It is not easy to acquire a boat in late spring nor is it easy to find the people to transform it into a seaworthy vessel. Everyone is too busy on the verge of the new tourist season. Also seeking a boat in the same port area near Athens, where *Dimitris K.* was, would arouse suspicions instantly. We had to go to a separate and unrelated place where Vangelis was also well known to the local people, because of his university and research activity.

A few days later we found a brilliant trehantiri, a traditional wooden fishing boat built by Euboean[4] ship builders. The vessel was afloat but had been abandoned for four years. The first inspection revealed rotten parts in the wooden framework. The boat needed to be moved to dry dock for repairs.

Our colleague, Thodoris was still one among few traditional craftsmen for wooden boats in Greece. He knew the *Agios Nikolaos*[5] very well. Unknown to him, this boat would become the *Liberty* of Free Gaza movement fame. He took great pride in it as he pulled it ashore. "It'll be ready next year, Vangelis," he said. Fair enough for such a busy boat builder looking forward to some rest in the upcoming heat of August.

But not fair enough for the Free Gaza mission. "Next year sounds too late. I need it ready in a month's time," Vangelis said, while smiling at Thodoris, his boat-building friend. There was no answer on the spot, but we were quite certain Thodoris and his coworkers would curse the Professor and his unreasonable demands.

After the boat accomplished its mission, Thodoris would later describe what exactly happened. "I was lying on the sofa watching TV. There was a news report about boats that had broken the blockade of Gaza. Suddenly, *Agios Nikolaos* was on the screen. I blinked. I couldn't believe my own eyes. I said to my wife, 'That's our boat, ain't it? Our own bloody boat!' Had Vangelis told me beforehand, I would've worked more intensely to get it ready earlier. Since it's for the Palestinians, we could have worked all through the night as well."

Many of those people repairing the boat really did work very hard, even late into the night. There were of course some who were used to working rather slowly—taking long breaks for a pint of beer and chitchat at the café. There were moments

---

[4] Euboea is an Island Northeast of Athens where *Agios Nikolaos (The Liberty)* was hidden in dry-dock and launched.
[5] "Saint Nicolas" in Greek

during this time of secrecy and effort when Vangelis was on the brink of cardiac arrest.

How could you explain to the boatyard repairmen that they had to rush, knowing only that the Professor wanted the boat for a cruise with a bunch of friends from abroad? Could they have worked overtime at night then? But they did work overtime, as if they vaguely suspected that Vangelis wanted the boat for something more important, although he wouldn't tell them exactly what for.

Greta

While Vangelis and his Greek crew were getting the boats ready, Sharyn, Mary, Renee, Paul and I were busy trying to sort out the passenger list. Mary, with her extensive background in PayPal dealings, was taking care of the donations coming in. Paul knew a friend, who was an accountant and lawyer, and he filed for a 501C3 for us in the U.S. Amazingly, we got it in mid 2007.

Finally, in early 2008, we started to put a passenger list together. At one point, we had 88 people who said they wanted to go. By the time we arrived in Cyprus in August 2008, we had almost halved that number to 48. In that group were Lauren Booth, Yvonne Ridley, Jeff Halper from the Israeli Committee Against Home Demolitions, Hedy Epstein, an 84 year-old Holocaust survivor, Sister Anne Montgomery at 81 years old, a Greek member of Parliament, two Palestinians from Gaza and journalists from Ramattan and Al Jazeera.

The rest of us were long-time activists for Palestine, having been in Gaza or the occupied West Bank. We were teachers, lawyers, students, businesswomen, writers, medical personnel, religious people, and retired. Our ages ranged from 22 to 84, and we hailed from 17 countries. What held us together was a passionate commitment to justice for Palestine and opening the sea to the imprisoned people of Gaza.

Thinking we would leave at the end of July, I ordered all passengers to come into Cyprus on July 28 for training. Boy, were we in for a shock.

Bill Dienst, MD, July 26-29

I am on my way out— Boarding the plane in Spokane, Washington, I see a young man sporting a DARE T-shirt: Drug Abuse Resistance Education. Many of us need to project a message when we are traveling. No doubt I will project a message, too, when I come home.

Right now, while outbound, I wear no messages; I have to be careful. I am joining a movement of international activists who will attempt to break the Israeli-imposed siege of Gaza. We will sail two small wooden boats through international waters and directly into Gaza territorial waters. We'll sail right past the Israeli Navy, which keeps the people of Gaza trapped within their enclave, and into Gaza. It sounds crazy, I know. No boats have entered Gaza Port from international waters since Israel began occupying Gaza forty-one years ago.

This siege against the people of Gaza is supported by the USA and it EU allies; yet few in the West are even aware of this man-made humanitarian catastrophe. The goal of the Free Gaza movement is to raise world awareness of this fact.

I fly on to Denver and then an all-night flight that puts me in Frankfurt, Germany at noon the following day. From the airport, I take a train. Overloaded with luggage, I stumble out of the Hauptbahnhof, the main train station, and into the city.

I've got jet lag; my body hurts all over, and I'm stressing out with fear about our mission. I need to chill; I am a bit prone to emotionality right now, because this may prove to be a dangerous mission.

July 30, Larnaca Airport, Cyprus

At baggage claim, there are arrivals from Frankfurt, Tel Aviv, Beirut, Amman, and the Persian Gulf. Cyprus is a freewheeling, wide-open, anything-goes island divided into a Greek and a Turkish republic; it's the Bahamas of the eastern Mediterranean and a sort of Switzerland—a neutral party in the wider Middle East. It is also an offshore tax shelter for the wealthy and fifteenth in GNP among the world's nations.

Cyprus was a former British colony from 1917 until 1960. They drive on the left side of the road here. It still has British bases that are considered sovereign territory of the UK; it has been separated by an iron curtain into a Greek side and a Turkish side since 1974.

Donna Wallach, a fifty-seven-year-old Jewish-American meets me at the airport. She is wearing a Palestinian kefiyyeh and holding a sign that says Free Gaza movement. Donna lived in Israel for fifteen years, which she calls Occupied Palestine. She also has Israeli citizenship and is anti-Zionist.

An hour later, Scott Kennedy, from the Resource Center for Creative Nonviolence in Santa Cruz, California arrives. I met Scott for the first time in November 2006 in Gaza while we were witnessing Israeli tanks and Apache assault helicopters attack communities in Northern Gaza and kill scores of people. That November, Scott and I traveled together to the southern border town of Rafah, surrounded by a Palestinian Authority armed convoy. This convoy's mission was to protect us from the fact that we were from the United States.

After clearing the airport, we make it to an apartment just south of Larnaca Airport. It is hot and sweaty in late July. I attempt a fitful and futile overheated sleep. At 3:00 am Greta Berlin, Hedy Epstein, and Mary Hughes arrive from London. Hedy Epstein is an eighty-four-year-old Holocaust survivor who was born in Germany and escaped the Nazis as a child. Her entire family was exterminated. She holds the Nazis responsible for this; not the Palestinians, who had were not responsible in any way for the Holocaust. She is an anti-Zionist, pro-Palestinian supporter.

We talk orientation and logistics. Courtney Sheetz, a young student activist from New York, helps me through the confusion of mobile phones and SIM cards. We prepare coffee and breakfast; my futile attempts at sleep have turned into another all-nighter. At 7:15 A.M. Greta and I return to the airport and take an Olympic Airlines flight from Cyprus to Athens, Greece for a press conference to announce that the boats are on the way, and we are getting ready to go to Gaza.

We fly over the Greek islands. Greece has thousands upon thousands of kilometers of coastline and coves, which is good for us. Our two boats are hiding somewhere down there. The Israeli newspapers Ha'aretz and the Jerusalem Post are reporting that Israeli government officials are frustrated because they cannot find our boats. We had announced they were in Egypt, and who knows how much money they have spent trying to find them so they can destroy them and put an end to our mission before it begins.

The Israeli press is describing us as a group of "left wing radicals." It's laughable.

Let's see: Greta Berlin works as a media/presentation consultant for oil companies. Mary Hughes is a member of the Writer's Guild in Los Angeles, a licensed pilot, and a proud grandmother. David Schermerhorn is a retired NYC film producer and an experienced deckhand.

A bunch of radicals? Anne Montgomery is a Catholic nun and daughter of a U.S. admiral. I am the son of a U.S. Air Force colonel and a family doctor in a rural town in the Okanogan Valley of Washington State. There is much more to our group than Israeli stereotypes would like you to believe.

We have civil engineers, attorneys, teachers, electricians, journalists, postal workers, information technology experts, experienced Greek mariners, a chemist, a member of the Greek

Parliament, and more among our passengers. And yes, we have many people with years of experience in nonviolent direct action.

Some have been to Gaza before but most have not. Some have volunteered with the International Solidarity Movement (ISM). Some have been arrested and deported by Israel for being human rights activists. Some have been denied entry into Israel—not because we are violent, but because we are nonviolent, which is even more threatening to the Israeli occupiers who want to paint the entire Palestinian resistance movement as violent terrorists. Yep, if we are a bunch of left-wing radicals, we certainly have our share of talented people.

Some passengers and land crew waiting for the boats.
Bottom left to right: Huwaida Arraf, Sister Anne Montgomery, Mary Hughes Thompson, Donna Wallach, and Renee Bowyer. Top, Ren Tawil, Edith Lutz, Tom Nelson, Kathleen Wang, Scott Kennedy, Hedy Epstein, Monir Deeb, David Halpin, MD

Our Greek Partners on board the Liberty.
Front: Yiannis Karipidis, Nikolas Bolos, Paul Larudee, Co-Founder,
Petros Giotis. Back: Panagiotis Politis, Anastasios Kourakis, MP
(Thessaloniki, Greece) and Vangelis Pissias.

Chapter 4: Athenian Spooks

Sharyn Lock, Greta Berlin, Free Gaza media team, Bill Dienst,
Petros Giotis

Sharyn, July 28

Here's how we are being covered in the Israeli newspaper
Ha'aretz. They and we will know more tomorrow! I like how
they (pretend to) think we'd prefer a fight rather than actually
to achieve our aims.[1]

> Israel fears European ship may sail to Gaza to "break siege"
> By Barak Ravid
>
> Israel is worried by reports that a group of leftwing activists
> from Europe plan to set sail for Gaza from Cyprus on August
> 5 under the slogan Breaking the siege.
>   The activists will reportedly include three members of the
> European Parliament. It is still not certain how serious the
> plans are. However, Israel fears that if the ship does sail, it will
> create a provocation that would at best cause public relations
> damage and could even result in violence.
>   The Free Gaza movement and the International Solidarity
> Movement are organizing the ship. Many of the latter's
> members have been barred from entering Israel on security
> grounds.
>   The organizers have reportedly raised almost $300,000 to
> finance the operation and recruited sixty people to sail with
> the ship. These include activists from several countries as well
> as journalists.
>   According to the Free Gaza movement's Web site, the
> activists will include a Holocaust survivor, a survivor of the
> Palestinian Nakba, as Palestinians call Israel's creation in 1948,
> and other members of the Palestinian diaspora, in addition to
> the European parliamentarians.

According to the Web site, the plan is for the boat to enter Gaza's territorial waters—and, more specifically, the "special security zone" that the Israel Navy has declared off-limits to all boats. The organizers thereby hope to provoke a clash with the navy that will end with them being forcibly arrested.

An Israeli government source said that Israel still has little information about the plan, and it is not clear whether it will ever come off. A year ago, he noted, Israel received reports of a similar plan, but because of logistical difficulties the initiative never got off the ground.

In conversations with their Israeli counterparts, Cypriot officials have expressed concern about the boat departing from their shores but say they can do nothing to prevent it. According to the information that has reached Israel, however, Cyprus is not the only point of departure under consideration; the ship might also sail from Turkey or from Alexandria, Egypt.

Israel is still trying to discover the ship's exact identity and more details about the organizers' intentions. It is also trying to decide how to respond. One option that has been raised in official discussions is to simply allow the ship to reach Gaza and thereby foil the organizers' apparent desire for a clash.

Greta

In Cyprus, we were busy organizing a press conference, fielding questions from the Cypriot government about exactly when we were going and organizing the passengers. We were pretty sure we'd be ready to go by August 8 and were worried that our departure would coincide with the opening of the Olympic Games and our journey with our small boats would be lost in the news. We were wrong on both counts.

Ramzi, Renee, Mary and I decided it was time for a press conference. We needed to keep the momentum going, and the people in Cyprus were beginning to hear about us. We might as well announce the sailing

For Immediate Release
Can unarmed seaborne civilians break the siege of Gaza?

A press conference at 13:00 H, Tuesday, July 29 International Press Center, Athens Inaugurating the Free Gaza movement Sailing to Gaza

In August, unarmed Palestinians, Israelis, and internationals will sail directly to Gaza without going through Israeli territory and without seeking permission from Israeli authorities. They include an eighty-one-year-old Catholic nun, an eighty-four-year-old Holocaust survivor, Palestinians from Gaza, sixteen nationalities, members of at least four major religions, and the international press.

On Tuesday, July 29, 2008, the Free Gaza movement publicly introduces its international team along with the Greek vessels that will take volunteers from Cyprus to Gaza in popular solidarity with Palestinian human rights. From that day, any attempt to damage the project will be considered an act of aggression against a nonviolent international human rights mission.

The boats will stop at Greek ports to receive supporters, and there will be opportunities for the press and public figures to travel part of the way on board and to broadcast from aboard ship with the latest high-speed satellite data systems.

Sharyn, somewhere in the Med

We hope this press conference gives our beautiful boats a little more protection. The last few days, with no one knowing about the project here, felt quite risky. If anything happened, would anyone care much? It was hard to feel the boats were safe if we took our eyes off them for even a moment. Now it's public knowledge, so there will be interest (and perhaps some Greek sense of ownership of the mission), and we think that may give us a little more protection. The press conference was apparently packed! Someone we are working with keeps saying,

"If there is an attack on the boats, it should be seen as an act of war against Greece!" The specific location of the boats is still secret though.

According to my colleague Paul, there've been several attempts to obstruct the project. First, earlier this year, we almost bought a boat. The owner agreed, but then stopped communicating with us, and we were told the boat had been removed from the market. Was this the result of pressure from some hostile source? Maybe.

Next, our Israeli participants were indirectly informed that, should they travel with us, they might be charged with treason; a twenty-year sentence. Some of them understandably decided they would have to choose the land-team role instead of sailing and risking this. However, Jeff Halper said, "What the hell. "I'm going anyway. Let them try to charge me."

Then there was the Al Jazeera ad that wasn't. A donor specifically gave money for us to get an Al Jazeera ad produced and aired. This would have probably completely sorted out our funding deficits (currently we're going ahead partly on debt and faith!). Al Jazeera at first said they thought the ad was great, that they'd give us bonus airtime, the best slots, and then they didn't invoice us.

When we got them to answer our e-mails, they said new and various random things about how it wasn't quite right for airing, and if we said we'd solve the problems they mentioned, they immediately came up with new ones. The thing is, Al Jazeera needs access to Palestine, and you know who gives them that. Apparently there was a point when BBC journalists decided not to cooperate with the vetting Israel requires on some of their work, and for six months they weren't allowed into Palestine. Our best guess is this sort of pressure occurred.

Dr. Bill around Athens, July 29-August 7

Paul Larudee meets Greta and me at the Athens Airport. A taxi takes us to the International Press Center in Athens, where Paul and Greta launch into a press conference with local Greek colleagues translating in Greek. This is intended as a beginning of an intense burst of a major international media campaign. For this will be our main defense as unarmed civilians going up against the Israeli military and related spy agencies. The Greek press, along with Al Jazeera, and the Independent of London are all at the conference.

We intend to have international media aboard the boats; endorsements from international organizations are accelerating. Later, I meet my roommates—Osama is Palestinian from a village between Qalqilya and Tulkarem in the West Bank. He is separated from his family in the West Bank and is living in exile in London because of his previous political activism on behalf of Palestinian civil rights. He is an accomplished filmmaker and yet is not even thirty years old. He carries about five mobile phones that ring continuously. The requirements of his position keep him in a constant state of mania.

Osama talks on the phone with his young sister in the West Bank, whom he cannot see and cannot visit. The Israelis have forbidden him to return home. Osama's colleague is Christos, a Greek cameraman from the Macedonian province of Greece, who is also living in London. Christos has good information technology skills, and he, along with Darlene Wallach, figure out how to hook up my laptop to the Internet.

Darlene Wallach is Donna Wallach's identical twin sister. She is also an anti-Zionist, who lives in San Jose, California. She has an information technology background. She is sent out with others to work on the communication's equipment on the *Liberty*, which is hidden in an undisclosed port under a Greek name outside Athens.

70

Now we are living in a secret hideaway in a residential apartment in Athens, while the tenants are off on vacation in the Greek islands; it will become known affectionately as the Speakeasy also known as the Bat Cave, since it is deep inside an apartment block on the far side of a courtyard from the street, and one must pass through three steel doors to reach it.

Another hideaway that shelters fellow activists, Paul and Sharyn, is a few blocks away. I will call it the Safe House. The four-star hotel named the Zafolia becomes our meeting place during the following days.

Sharyn is based in Athens and is traveling back and forth to the boats. The *Free Gaza* is hidden away in a different port than the *Liberty*. That way, if one boat becomes discovered and sabotaged by Israeli intelligence, Mossad, there is always a second boat in a separate undisclosed harbor.

We meet with Vangelis, who along with several of his Greek colleagues found us the two boats we are using after Riad's suicide meant we had to start all over again. It becomes clear that many have committed their hearts, monies and souls into this project.

I also meet Ken O'Keefe, who has run a dive shop in Hawaii and worked as a human rights activist both in Iraq and in the West Bank. Ken is a former U.S. marine and has become an Irish citizen in an act of conscious protest of the current predatory U.S. foreign policy. We eat, drink, and talk late into the night below the ancient Acropolis, getting to know each other while addressing logistics about how we might pull off our high-risk, quixotic plan.

We haven't left for Cyprus just yet; we are behind schedule by two weeks. Even though we initially projected a departure from Cyprus on August 8, we are far from being ready. It's always more complicated than it initially seems. Greek maritime inspectors must declare the boats seaworthy, and since they are old fishing vessels, they need a major tune-up before they are shipshape.

71

Additionally, we have information technology experts who are part of our crew. They are installing a sophisticated communications system capable of broadcasting real-time images to shore via the Internet. That way, if the Israeli Navy tries to play rough with us, a group of unarmed nonviolent human rights activists, the whole world will be watching…we hope.

I spend my time trying to develop liaisons with Greek politicians and health care personnel. My goal is to acquire medical equipment and pharmaceutical supplies in two categories:

1. Medical supplies for the besieged hospitals and health care workers in Gaza. Of course, our efforts are only a small drop in the bucket; our two small boats cannot bring sufficient supplies for 1.5 million people who are under this cruel siege. What we take is symbolic only, our major objective is to challenge Israel's illegal siege on Gaza. But we will do what we can.

2. Medical supplies for the boat crew and passengers. Since we face the real possibility of being attacked, we must plan as best we can for the worst while hoping for the best. We don't have the resources to stock a fully equipped sickbay or a hospital ship. The best we can do is to be prepared to provide first aid for common medical ailments, while stabilizing more seriously ill medical or surgical patients before transferring them by air or boat to shore.

We must have supplies to provide trauma first aid in the event that we are attacked. If that happens, we might also have to plan for massive evacuation, which is problematic. The nearest shore for evacuation for most of our journey will be hospitals in Israel, the country most likely to attack us. Other alternatives would be Cyprus, Lebanon, or Egypt. If the Israelis evacuate us, they could then try to spin this into some kind of a propaganda victory about rescuing "those naïve fools at sea."

We have already required all of our boat passengers to obtain medical evacuation insurance before coming on this voyage. We are told in these insurance policies that our evacuation insurance is not applicable in a war zone. Fortunately neither Gaza nor Israel nor the international waters around them have been classified as a war zone. (This must come as great relief to Gaza residents who have been through numerous assaults from Israeli F-16s, tanks, and Apache attack helicopters over the past several years.)

If we do have a medical emergency, if we are attacked or have some other disaster at sea, we will have to see if our insurers will honor our policies and pay for our evacuations. Still, this is the best that we can do to mitigate the financial effects of any disaster that might happen to us.

Sharyn, August 2

First, I stayed in Athens, where our main Greek contact's wider political circle had volunteered for the job of hosting us, insisting on paying for anything we might attempt to buy, and seeking out obscure things (like helium canisters for balloons) that we wanted. I immediately felt so very welcome and supported on this mad mission.

There I met our quietly spoken, awesomely on-the-case contact, Vangelis, who had put a level of effort into procuring and preparing our boats that I still haven't really got my head round. We'll buy boats, we said, as if it was like buying shoes. Ha! We had NO IDEA. Thank God he did, and instead of telling us how impossible it was to find, buy, renovate, equip, license, and crew two boats in the height of national summer holiday, simply went about doing it.

These people! I don't dare think of this as "my" project anymore. I am not one of the people who have for weeks begun work daily at 6:00 A.M., labored hard in the Greek summer sun, and skipped the afternoon break that's supposed to prevent you dying of heat exhaustion; people who've literally been unable to sleep for worry about engines, bridges, and the uneven flow of money from us to pay for anything. They didn't even know who the hell we were at first and didn't care because it was Gaza they were working for anyway. Even now, all I can do is paint bits of boat for them and in between painting things, beam at these good hardworking folks and buy them the odd beer.

Back to my reward, only half of which is meeting my comrades. The other half is that this is all taking place on a small Greek island that doesn't allow cars—only mopeds, one of which we have hired and I drive gleefully with no helmet (sorry, Dad, I don't think they sell them here). After boat work and computer work, there is the bright sea to dive in and in all of this I am in the company of Vittorio, my tall, dark, handsome Italian colleague.

A few days ago, we sat up with our boat into the early hours, at the whitewashed bar opposite, under the stars. We were counting down the hours until the boats' Greek presence was announced, until which they were more vulnerable.

Apart from diving into the sea with my camera and my phone in my pockets (one phone down, two to go), and a cash-flow problem that had me phoning anyone I knew that could maybe lend us something toward a late €10,000 that was about to set off a domino effect of delays, everything has been going well. Tomorrow I must go back to Athens to follow up various loose ends and boss people round.

I heard that one of the Athens anarchists has made me an anarchy flag to fly. How sweet is that?

Petros, Launching the *Agios Nikolaos* (*Liberty*)

Work was in progress and the deadline was drawing near. Then Vangelis set the deus ex machina working, as in the ancient Greek tragedies.

The deus ex machina was Markos, a six-foot-ten, half-Greek, half-Norwegian lad: a physicist who had studied in the United States and Norway, a diver, a seaman, a captain, an electronics expert and an inventor. He had an incredible combination of skills and knowledge. Vangelis decided to include him and he responded, "Why didn't you tell me before so that I wasn't so busy in August and could travel with you to Gaza?"

Markos immediately started working. He coordinated the different working groups and worked directly on individual projects, as well. At the same time, we thought that I should appear in the Greek port of Eretria outside of Athens, where the boat was being hidden, and be prepared to give a hand. A number of foreign and Greek friends were already working there and guarding the boat. I took on the task of transporting the materials needed from Athens.

Markos would give me the list of supplies, and every morning I bought them from shops in Piraeus and carried them to Eretria, sometimes in my car and sometimes using the van of a comrade. It was really a "welcome-to-the-madhouse" situation. Imagine me, a bearded journalist smoking a pipe, buying boat material in shops, without knowing much of anything of boats and related stuff! The shop owners in Piraeus were immediately curious about what I was up to, so I had to make up a story! I told them that I was a writer who was going on a research mission sponsored by the Institute of Underwater Archeological Research. I wanted to write a book and at the same time would be helping them in the preparation of their boat.

In the shops in the small village of Eretria, I changed roles. There, I appeared as a polytechnic professor, an associate of Vangelis, whom they already knew. I could have been of some technical help concerning the ship but preferred to be back and forth on the street. I will confess to something: I preferred going back home to Athens, rather than being near the ship and sleeping there.

Still, I was haunted by the thought that something could go wrong and the boat might not be seaworthy enough in time to make the voyage to Gaza. Each day, early in the afternoon, I would reach Eretria, driving a loaded car onto the ferry and hoping to finally see the boat in the water as I crossed. Seeing that it was still under repair in the dry dock day after day, I was growing increasingly uncomfortable.

All that went on until one night when we were finally informed that the next day the boat was to be definitely launched. That following day I arrived early in the afternoon. In my car with me were Courtney and Dr. Bill. I was sure that the boat would have been launched by the time we arrived.

I was stunned to see it hadn't moved from the spot where it had been sitting on blocks for weeks while it had been under repair. I found Nikos Bolos, our captain, swimming with O.J., one of the crewmembers, below the hull of the boat. I was a bit angry.

"You are swimming while the boat is still on land?" I asked. I must have been impossible. Nikos calmly explained that the heat had melted the wooden drivers, which meant that the planned noon launching had failed. So they decided to launch it at six in the evening, when the temperature was lower. Indeed, that evening Theodoris and his apprentices arrived, and they initiated the preparations in the usual gregarious Greek way—with a lot of shouting and swearing.

They asked us to board the boat, so that they could launch it properly. I was too anxious to do that, so I remained on the shore with Courtney, who would film the launching, and Fatua,

Ken's wife, who was pregnant and should not take any chances.

The vessel started smoothly sliding down the wooden drivers until it finally splashed the water's edge—a beautiful sight! Costas was in his own boat, guiding the launch from a little farther out at sea, just in case. For a short time, we wondered whether its engine would start. Then suddenly it coughed, and roared into action.

Nikos gestured from the bridge that everything was going swimmingly. The boat turned slowly and headed for the harbor. We were tip-top happy! We jumped into the car and drove around the harbor to meet the boat as it docked at the quay.

There was a lot of tension during the next three days. The mechanic attended to the final details. A lot of the electrical work had to be completed. I put on overalls and started working as Markos's helper. We had to call in Lefteris, an electrician who worked late into the night. Niognomon carried out the last checks, and it was decided that we would definitely be leaving on the 8th of August on our way to Cyprus. But that would be impossible.

On the previous day, Takis Politis, a university professor, and Yiannis Karipidis, a film director, arrived to join the mission. Everybody was absolutely ready. Markos gathered us all and told us about teamwork onboard the boat. Simple rules, including the food we have, how we stand and work on the deck, and how to react to a distress situation.

Greta, University of Nicosia, Cyprus, August 5

Thirty-two passengers and ten members of the land crew were now waiting… and waiting… and waiting for the boats. The others were on the boats… somewhere. We had no idea where the crew and passengers were or even if there were any boats. Every day, I received a phone call from Paul or Vangelis or

Sharyn. "Yes, we're on the way. We promise we're on the way soon." Little did any of us know that it would be another two weeks before the boats would appear in Cyprus.

We were staying at the University of Cyprus campus in Nicosia, and the average daytime temperature was hovering at 100^0 F with no air conditioning in our rooms. There were hundreds of cats wandering the grounds, thin and feral, and, of course, we Americans wanted to feed them and adopt them. Two activists actually thought they would smuggle a few cats on board the boats... just in case there were any mice. They whined and meowed all day and all night.

We met every day in the large student headquarters, fortunately the only place on campus with air conditioning. Many of us who had suffered through the heat in Hebron or Jenin or Ramallah had a hard time in Nicosia. It was odd, we could put up with discomfort in occupied Palestine but not in Nicosia.

And, those of us who were the primary organizers had to keep the passengers busy. We were already late by a week. So Ramzi Kysia, Tom Nelson and I cooked up an idea that we would write to Tzipi Livni and invite her to go with us to see the damage the Israeli military had done to the people of Gaza. We thought it a brilliant idea. The three of us lay out under the Cypriot moon one night and composed the following press release:

5 August 2008, Tzipi Livni Foreign Affairs Minister, Israel

Dear Foreign Minister Livni

On behalf of the Free Gaza movement, we would like to formally invite you to join us on our upcoming voyage from Cyprus to the Gaza Strip. We feel that your presence on this important mission would help alleviate concerns that have been expressed in the Israeli media about our objectives. More importantly, we believe that it would be extremely helpful for you to see firsthand the horrific effects of Israeli policies on the people of the Gaza Strip, as well as to witness firsthand the effectiveness of nonviolent action in bringing about positive change.

While we disagree with many of the statements and policies you have made as the Israeli Foreign Minister, we wholeheartedly agree with a portion of something you wrote two years ago when you said:

"For too long, the Middle East has been governed by zero-sum logic. One side's loss was seen as the other's gain. This thinking has brought much suffering to our region" (Tzipi Livni, "The Peace Alternative," Asharq Alawsat, 18 June 2007).

This is absolutely correct. We seek an end to this suffering. We find ourselves, and you must be feeling this intensely yourself, in truly difficult times. The one thing that is clear is that violence has not worked for anyone in this conflict. As a group of avowed nonviolent, peace activists, we hope that you will accept this opportunity, move past the zero-sum logic of your government's blockade, and join us on this historic voyage to break the siege of Gaza.

Your government's siege on the people of Gaza has been deemed illegal by numerous human rights organizations, has lead to the death of over 200 patients in the last year as a result of being denied adequate medical care, and has caused a man-made humanitarian catastrophe in the Gaza Strip. Clearly this is not the behavior of a civilized government, nor can these policies ever lead to peace for Israel.

Our voyage may seem to be a quixotic endeavor and therefore easily dismissed, but as a group of individuals who fervently believe that such moves can be vitally transforming and that individuals do indeed have the power to change our world for the better, we hope that you will take our offer seriously. We set sail for Gaza in the next few days. Please join us.

Sincerely Yours, The Steering Committee for the Free Gaza movement, Cyprus

Well, all hell broke loose when this email went out. Half the passengers thought it was a brilliant idea, half thought we were insane and sucking up to the Israelis. The Greeks were furious that we were even considering communication with Israel, one of the many times that our different cultures got in the way. They didn't understand the irony of what we were doing by forcing Israel to answer us. We weren't asking for permission to go to Gaza, we were inviting Tipsy (that's what we had nicknamed her) to come along to witness the devastation in Gaza.

It turned out that the Israeli government was more worried about us than we were about them. They actually responded, stating,

> We know you are good people, but you are misguided. There is already a process to transfer goods from charities into Israel.

When we pointed out that they made a huge mistake by saying there was a process to transfer goods from us to Israel… and not Gaza, we all thought it was a marvelous Freudian slip. In the long run, our attempt at keeping the mission on the front page was tremendously successful, thanks to Israel's faux pas.

Of course, we were not going to Gaza to deliver goods, even though a small portion of our cargo was hearing aids and toys for children. We were going to Gaza to break Israel's illegal blockade on the people there.

Renee and I had been teachers in a former life, and, like teachers, we wanted to keep people busy. We bought paint and canvas and markers, and then set the passengers to work making huge banners for the boats. Every night, the lights from the dorm would shine down on the busy artists who made everything from Handalas to Arabic sayings for the side of the boats. Keeping them busy during the day, however, in the heat and the frustration was an entirely different matter.

Dr. Bill, August 5-7

During my final two days in Greece, I am at last taken to one of the boats, the *Liberty*, which is hidden in a harbor that is about a two-hour drive and then a short ferry ride across a cove from Athens. The *Liberty* is still in dry dock when I arrive, but several hours later, it is launched and taken around to the end of the marina inside the breakwater; now we can walk to town and the ferry dock, which we can see in the distance.

We don't want the villagers at these hidden ports to become suspicious about what we are planning. Even though the majority of Greeks sympathize with the Palestinian cause, gossip among villagers could wind up being passed along to the wrong people.

We pretend that we are a crew of marine biologists about to embark on a research excursion. We are warned by Vangelis not to talk about our real mission, even among ourselves if others can hear us, as some of the villagers can understand English. For Gaza, we say Mikonos, a Greek Island and tourist destination. We try our best, but several of us slip up periodically and mention the G-word.

During the next few days, it will become one of my jobs to mediate conflicts between the people working and traveling on the boats. Without taking sides, let me just state the obvious: A mission such as the Free Gaza movement attracts folks who are hardheaded, independent-minded, stubborn and ingenious individuals. With all these attributes comes an ego. We all tend to be opinionated and to no one's surprise, sometimes see the world differently.

It is a very interesting social experiment we have created: you put different kinds of people united by a human rights cause on a couple of boats together and add a bunch of logistical hurdles, different cultures, different nationalities, different languages and customs, and then add deadlines and fear, paranoia and stress. There is bound to be conflict, the patterns are almost predictable.

Over time, several of us are charged with mediating these multiple conflicts, so that our differences do not overcome our common mission; after all, we can't let these differences degenerate and turn us into a ship of fools. I admit that this will result in several of us driving each other nuts over several occasions.

At nightfall I wander into town to have dinner and a look around. Walking back to the boat, I wind up getting lost. At the breakwater, where I think the boat is located I can't figure out which boat it is in the dark. As I wander back toward town, a camper is parked strategically on the shoreline at the entrance to the boat dock.

Children are playing around the camper and a woman jumps out and asks if she can help. I explain that I am lost. I walk back to town and find my shipmates, who drive me right back to the boat; I had walked right past the boat, but I just didn't recognize it in the dark.

During the night we sleep in shifts, with each person taking turns at a two-hour watch. My shift is between 2:00 and 4:00 A.M. Headlights approach our boat along the quay and fear builds inside me as each car approaches. I suppress the urge to cry wolf as the cars pass by. I don't want to wake up the sleeping crew, who are already exhausted, needlessly.

I spend the next two days with my shipmates hauling supplies from town to the boat. As I walk to the junction between the breakwater and the shore, I pass the camper. This same woman, whom I saw before the previous night when I was lost, jumps out and asks me if I found my boat. I respond, "Yes."

"So where is it?" she asks. She is in her early forties or late thirties. She is attractive, with long black hair. She could be Greek or she could be Israeli. "Up the breakwater a ways," I respond vaguely. There is something intriguing about this woman and this camper.

In the ensuing days, I noticed that all of the camper windows are occluded by sun-block reflectors. Of course, it's a hot Greek summer day. So I can't be sure whether my concerns about espionage are legitimate. Maybe they are just trying to keep their camper from overheating in the August sun. Though I try, I can never get a decent look at what's inside the camper when I pass by.

I pass again from the boat walking atop the breakwater. As I pass the camper parked at the shore entrance, the woman jumps out behind me. I turn around and have a good look at her, say nothing and then walk on. I wonder if I should greet her with "Shalom!" the next time I see her.

I pass from town carrying supplies and walk back along the breakwater toward the boat. As I pass by, I see a man in scuba gear getting out of the water alongside the camper. This sets off alarms, because it does not look like Ken. He is the one who scuba dives and inspects the bottom of the boat each day to make sure it has not been sabotaged from underneath. So who is this man?

The *Liberty* is planning to leave this port for Crete as soon as we pass the Greek maritime inspectors' evaluations. The first evaluation, conducted the previous night, uncovered a few flaws when our captain operated the boat at full throttle. These deficits need to be corrected, so we are stuck here for a few more days, all of us becoming more and more paranoid. We have heard from the organizers in Cyprus that they are getting phone calls saying things like, "There is a bomb on board your boats," and "Do you know how to swim?"

I am looking forward to sailing to Crete aboard the *Liberty*, the sooner the better. But just then I get a call from Paul Larudee, who is either in Athens or with the *Free Gaza*. I can't ask him where he is because someone might be listening to our phone conversation or trying to pinpoint our locations by GPS.

"Bill, you need to fly back to Cyprus tomorrow. The boat passengers staying at the university are going stir-crazy waiting for the boats. They don't understand the problems we're having here. They are about to have a mutiny. So I need you to fly back to give them an update from the perspective of someone who has actually been out to one of the boats. And I need you to teach your trauma first aid course that you have prepared for them."

"Okay," I answer. I guess I won't be sailing to Crete after all. Before returning to Athens, I discreetly report my suspicions about the Mossad camping van parked at the foot of the breakwater entrance, including my spotting of the scuba diver.

"Are you sure?" Giorgos asks me.

"How can I be sure?" I answer. "It looks a little fishy to me. Just keep an eye on them."

When I get back to the boat, I point out the camper on the shoreline to Vangelis.

"I think they are Mossad," I say.

If the Israelis can disable the vessels while minimizing human casualties, it would be the best way out for them. If they maim or kill unarmed international human rights activists, it becomes more of a public relations disaster. As I take the ferry back across the bay toward Athens, I take pictures of our ship on the dock and the suspected camper/spy-mobile.

Adam Qvist, our youngest passenger from Denmark, is writing out the Arabic for the banners.

Chapter 5: Are We There Yet? Waiting for the Boats in Cyprus

Mary Hughes Thompson, Sharyn Lock, Bill Dienst, Petros Giotis, Paul Larudee, Greta Berlin, Yvonne Ridley, Aki Nawaz, Donna Wallach

Mary Hughes Thompson, reflecting on the long days of waiting at the University of Cyprus in Nicosia

While in Cyprus, we were pretty much in hiding because we had very real fears that something could happen to one or more of us that would scuttle the entire project. Greta, Ramzi and I gave strict instructions to everyone that if they left the campus, they were to go in twos. We were constantly followed by two hippies who showed up everywhere we went. Strange characters were seen skulking about the campus late at night. We formed a night watch, kept all our doors locked and all our eyes open. There was a lot of apprehension, mostly because we were now tired and crabby with the heat and we were late leaving and most of us weren't even sure any longer that there were boats. But, so far, none of the passengers were leaving.

Sharyn, August 8

Dear Cyprus Passengers,

From this, you may deduce
1. I am not in any immediate danger.
2. I am under some stress!

Everything's taking us longer (and high sea winds are playing havoc with the schedule), but the whole thing's just getting bigger.

So you'll have heard about the strong winds that have

scuppered the current schedule. You should have seen our expressions when it was explained to us. We were not entirely sure that jumping off something very high was not a better option than phoning Greta at the University of Cyprus and breaking the news to passengers waiting there. I made Paul do it. Now I'm trying to write you some commiserations.

I know some of you have reasons that mean you might have to leave. All very well for me; my next appointment is a midwifery degree on September 22. I guess the reason I blocked out two months of my life is that, in my experience, delays for such complicated arrangements often happen. Ideally we will keep you all; I can't imagine how you will feel if you have to pack up and leave at this stage having not even seen a boat.

You have been part of this with us, and maybe for some people their contribution is to begin the public part of the project, to go home and continue to look after those of us who stay. From a two-year perspective in working on this project, the delay is a small blip in a big important plan—not for us but for Gaza. It's bigger than all of us now!

We're sending Dr. Bill back to tell you our beautiful boats DO exist and they DO move! I hope we don't have to lose a single one of you.

Dr. Bill, August 8-20

My plane leaves Athens in the evening and I enjoy the panoramic archipelago of Greek islands below one more time. This time I have a better appreciation for the history and geography of Greece than when I flew toward Athens a week and a half ago. I also have more of a clue about where our boats are and where they are going.

The next day I meet with a Cypriot doctor about acquiring medical supplies for the boats. We Americans forgot that August is not the right time to try and mobilize the acquisition of medical equipment on short notice in Greece or Cyprus. Everyone is either on vacation or about to go on vacation, including this doctor. I had tried to make contacts by e-mail from May until July before I arrived; but it still takes a personal touch to make things happen. It is becoming hard to make progress, especially when my answers to the question about our departure from Cyprus are, "I don't know exactly, but very soon."

I head inland to Nicosia to the University of Cyprus, where FG passengers have been assembling and participating in workshops. Immediately around us are real college students taking summer courses from Germany, Spain, Italy, Albania, Bulgaria, Egypt, and other countries. The campus is relaxed and not crowded this time of year. These students are intrigued to hear about our FG project and pleased to see older folks like us still acting out our ideals in a project like this. The evenings are a real social event, as we compare our perspectives on the world and compete with each others' musical tastes out in the courtyard in front of the main student center where the sound system is located.

Upon arrival, I enter a classroom workshop, one of many that have been in session during the previous days. Waiting can be the hardest part. The participants are indeed becoming stir-crazy and many people are getting on each other's nerves. This workshop is about jail solidarity—what to do if we are all collectively arrested at sea and jailed in Israel. Many of those sharing the classroom are veterans of the International Solidarity Movement and have done many nonviolent direct actions in defense of Palestinian people, mostly in the occupied West Bank, but some in Gaza.

Andrew Muncie and Theresa McDermott from Scotland have been arrested and deported from Israel for nonviolent direct action. Mary Hughes, Greta Berlin, and Maria Del Mar have all been seriously assaulted and injured by Israeli occupation forces.

Ramzi Kysia, the son of Lebanese parents from Washington, DC, is acting as facilitator at these meetings.

Aside from experiences in Lebanon, Ramzi has somehow talked his way into staying inside Kibbutz Barkai in Israel for five days with the family of a friend. He has also been in Iraq off and on between the years 2001 and 2003 doing the kind of nonviolent direct action work that he is doing with us now. He has an analytical mind that is as sharp as a tack, and he is a stickler for detail.

We have five Jews among our boat passengers; the Wallach sisters and Hedy Epstein. Edith Lutz is a former nurse and now educator from Germany. She joined this voyage to help children in Gaza and highlight the core of Jewish religion: love and humanity, not force and hatred.

Jeff Halper, who left us a few days ago for Crete, where he will meet up with the boats, is the only Israeli on the Free Gaza movement boats who is still living in Israel. In 2006, the American Friends Service Committee nominated Jeff to receive the 2006 Nobel Peace Prize with Palestinian intellectual and activist Ghassan Andoni.

Just before I arrived, Dr. David Halpin and his wife had left after teaching a sea safety course. Dr. Halpin is a British orthopedic surgeon who operates the Dove and Dolphin, which brings medical and other supplies to Gaza. Because of the siege, his supplies have had to go through the Israeli Port of Ashdod, about thirty kilometers north of the Gaza Strip and are then transported overland to Gaza, which adds expense and delay. They are examples of the tremendous support we were now getting from people around the world.

Among the Arab passengers are Ren Tawil, a second generation Palestinian-American from Minnesota, Monir Deeb, originally from Gaza and now living in Los Angeles, and Musheir El Farra, a civil engineer, also originally from Gaza but now living in Sheffield, England. Huwaida Arraf, a Palestinian-American lawyer who also has Israeli citizenship and teaches in Jerusalem is on one of the boats somewhere in the Mediterranean. She is a Co-Founder of the International

Solidarity Movement (ISM). We also have Fathi Joaudi, a cameraman from Tunis who has been following Musheir around taping him for a possible TV special. We never see Fathi without the camera attached to a wide belt around his waist, and even when we are all ultimately seasick on our way to Gaza, Fathi is still attached to that camera for dear life. Finally, we have Rashid, who works as a journalist for Arabic BBC in London and is originally from Algeria. Once we leave, they will be joined by a Palestinian cameraman from Ramattan as well as a Palestinian cameraman from Al Jazeera.

As facilitator, it is Ramzi's job to keep us focused on our mission. He must allow everyone a chance to be heard, while keeping the extroverts from monopolizing the proceedings. It is a thankless task, but Ramzi does a pretty good job. Each morning he gives us a typed summary of what we decided the previous day to see if we are still in agreement, and if not, he offers us the opportunity to refine the document further. This seems like endless tinkering with the messages to some, which adds to their stir craziness.

My presentations at these workshops are a little bit less mundane. I must give three one-hour sessions (over three days) in trauma first aid for the boat passengers who are interned here; transforming them from lay people into basic emergency trauma technicians able to cope as best they can with a mass casualty incident. One of my main jobs is to be the disaster planner for Free Gaza movement: plan for the worst while hoping for the best. After all, if the Israeli Navy really wants to, it has the clear capability to put torpedoes through both our boats and kill us all.

The fact that we represent seventeen different nationalities makes this a much more difficult option for the Israelis. My instruction to this group is intended to empower them, so that we can increase the likelihood that as many of the short-term survivors as possible can become long-term survivors and live to tell their tales. I also have to prepare them to function as best they can in the event that I and other health care providers are killed or incapacitated to the point where we can't help others who are wounded.

So after scaring the shit out of my colleagues, I try and cheer them up. On Saturday evening after dinner, we are scheduled to have the next day off. So, I play disc jockey and set up a dance party out in the courtyard as the sun goes down, the heat of the day dissipates, and the crescent moon rises over the college campus.

That night, the late night crew spots some suspicious individuals walking around on campus (we were staggering the watches as our trip was further and further delayed and more people realized where we were). They claim that they are architects, who were driving by from Larnaca and had just stopped because they "were impressed by the architecture"... at 3:00 am. Yeah, right.

They were referred to campus security but never showed up. Some of my friends tried to follow them, but they disappeared. Israeli spies? I don't know. But their behavior was certainly peculiar.

From Hidden Ports on Greek Mainland, through Aegean Waters to International Media Attention

Petros, August 8

Today is the day. A friend will drive me to Eretria at daybreak and get my car back to Athens. I packed a few things in a small bag but am feeling anxious that I have forgotten something. Luckily, I didn't forget my laptop, my cassette recorder, or my camera.

Giorgos wants to come and see the boat. On the ferry, we have a chat and arrange communication through the Internet.

I'll write a piece every day, and the comrades will upload them on our and other Web sites.

Everybody is asleep on the boat, except the night watchman. The crew and passengers have been on continuous watch at this stage, ever since the Agios Nikolaos (*Liberty*) was launched from its berth. I introduce Giorgos and Darlene; we talk for a while, then he leaves, and I start working. There are quite a few jobs to be completed—mainly things on deck involved with passenger comfort. On a fishing boat, you cannot expect to have many creature comforts. The day is feverish. Markos and I work on board and finish installation of lights. Ken deals with the rest of the woodwork. He is a real master of his craft. Darlene has a knack for the nitty-gritty and knows the location of all kinds of screws. We should be leaving today. Ken and I can look after the rest en route to Cyprus.

At noon we load foodstuffs, mainly water. Markos has doubled the quantity of estimated water needed. You can manage without food at sea but never without water. Markos and Nikos inform us, "You aren't sailors. The boat will be topsy-turvy even when the sea is calm, so mind what you are eating. You only need pretzels, cheese, olives, honey, and lots of water." These are Mediterranean products, actually. For more than three thousand years, local people have sailed the seas feeding on such blessed natural products.

Vangelis joins us at noon, smiling. He's got all the paperwork. The boat is legal and in his name. No Greek authority can stop us. It's been a real battle against red tape through various Greek governmental regulatory bureaus. Very few people could know what Vangelis has been through until he finally got all the paperwork. The rest had the simpleminded impression that they boarded two boats that were bought as if you were buying a couple of used cars. Our mission owes a lot to Vangelis, since he's been the coordinator of the operative aspect, the person who discovered, bought and changed two simple fishing boats into passenger-carrying vessels. He is the one who took all the risks—financial, political, and legal. Apart from traveling by ferry and in his car, he sometimes had to commute using buses in case he was being followed.

We were all later informed that Mossad spent a pretty penny in attempts to trace the boats; they searched in Cyprus, Turkey, Egypt, and Greece, but they found nada. Our boats were well hidden in two territorial shipyards and guarded by trusted people. The Zionists' money was spent in vain.

It was noon when we got the official departure document from the Eretria Port Police. Officially, Vangelis would be the captain as the owner of a private "entertainment boat." Vangelis himself had to leave the *Liberty* though, to inspect the departure of *Free Gaza* from Spetses Harbor. He will travel to Chania, Crete on it, where we will make our first stop and officially announce to the world that these are the boats that will be breaking the siege of Gaza. (We can finally brag a bit—can't we?) Even when the boats reach Chania, neither Mossad nor the Greek authorities will know about the mission. Our good-old clandestine methods have once again proven fruitful.

At 20:00 hours, when it is getting cooler, the *Liberty* pulls up anchor and starts out of the Gulf of Eretria heading south. Nikos Bolos is the captain, and Ken O'Keefe, the first mate. Markos and Nikos continue our intensive on-the-job training of the crew, as we are finally underway. Many of us, Greek and foreigner, are fast becoming sailors.

We are all exhausted but satisfied. The only things we worry about now are engine problems since this boat is sailing on a long voyage after many years. Not to worry, though. Nikos, a chemist by profession and able sailor, has sufficient knowledge of engine matters to act properly if need be. The route is also full of islands; we may go ashore and carry out further repairs if Nikos is unable to fix a problem. The trip to Chania would be the final test for the boat and will show us its weak points. Then we can act accordingly. After Crete, we have to sail in the open sea for two days to Cyprus and then it will take another day and a half to Gaza.

It is past midnight and we get near the bright lights of Rafina. The boat reduces speed, closes in on the pier, and Markos takes a leap onto the pier, without the boat even having to stop. That looks incredible to us land people; for we are not "sea wolves." I finally go to bed. The hum of the engine and the gentle rocking of the boat put me into a deep sleep.

Saturday, August 9

I wake up at six in the morning, make myself a cup of coffee, and go to the bridge. Takis Politis, our best steersman, is at the wheel. He doesn't make too many detours, which shortens our trip and more importantly lowers our fuel costs. Two hours later, I discover that we aren't getting any power from the engine generator. I wake Nikos.

He sees that the fan belt is . We hold a quick meeting and decide not to go ashore for repairs, so that we won't waste time getting to Crete (we are off the coast of Melos). We start up the mobile deck generator and presto! We have power on board again.

In the meantime, the GPS batteries are out, there is a wrong handling of things, and there's no way to steer the boat electronically. Nikos shows me how to sail using the compass—the good old traditional and reliable way of navigation for an experienced seaman. Later on, we radio the GPS manufacturer, and they give us explicit instructions on how to repair it.

We are having lovely weather. There's almost no wind. At times, a light north breeze pushes us on, increasing the speed to ten knots. We only want to use eight knots so as not to dodge the engine. Off the coast of Serifos, we see some Mediterranean dolphins. Two of them approach the boat swimming playfully. Nikos, who adores ancient Greek mythology, mentions Amphitrite dolphins (she was the wife of Poseidon, the Greek god of the sea). He starts whistling and the dolphins gather round the boat, jumping and diving all the time, while our foreign friends frantically take pictures and video them.

Well, the first serious mistake has been made: the deck generator, which was not intended for constant work, is now our primary power source. Two hours before arriving in Chania, it breaks down. Now we can only get power from the batteries, and we definitely must not turn on any lights, since the power supply is sufficient only for the boat dashboard on the bridge.

At 20:45, twenty-four hours after our departure, we reach the old harbor of Chania, which is an old Venetian-style harbor, probably the most beautiful one in Greece. We've made arrangements and people are expecting us. I phone Vangelis and I ask, "Do we sneak in, pretending to be unimportant, or do we raise the flag of our mission?" There are people on the shore who have worked in the repairing part of the mission, and up to this moment, don't have a clue about the destination of the boats. The official names for the Free Gaza movement boats were not to be announced and still carry their Greek name, another reason Mossad cannot find them. On the other hand, on the very next day we will be officially announcing that these are the boats that will try to break the siege of Gaza.

We decide to hang the banner of the mission over the back of the boats, thus making a giant leap from a covert operation into an overt proclamation. **Here We Come Mossad!** The sky is the limit.

At this point, an important issue that we'd dared not think about arises—we didn't have captains to sail such heavy wooden vessels.

Nikos does the sailing. He has sailed the Mediterranean in light sailing boats. He is qualified to pilot heavier fishing boats with a power engine but just barely. He could handle the situation while the boat was docking in the port of Eretria but only with delicate handling. He lacks the confidence of a more experienced power fishing boat pilot. In the case of the harbor of Chania, the boat has to enter prow first and maneuver between two other boats, just as you would park your car in a crowded parking area. But boats have no brakes.

The wheel does not respond well when we approach slowly and the reverse stern propulsion takes some time before it works, producing a frightening moment for everyone on the boat. This kind of a docking procedure does not present a real problem for a fishing boat captain, but for a person whose experience is with a light sailboat, this problem proves to be untenable. As a result, we on the *Liberty* became stranded on a shallow reef, just eighteen yards from the dock.

Relief finally follows our general panic and grief. While we are frantically trying to figure things out, our friends on the shore keep phoning us. They can see us, but they cannot understand why we have stopped, what is happening. The issue is whether we should abandon the boat. I intervene calmly but decidedly, saying, "We don't abandon ship. We are going for a walk now, through one of the most beautiful Greek cities, so everyone just relax. Tomorrow we will fix any problems with the ship." We decide to ferry ourselves to shore using the small rubber motorboat called a Zodiac. We leave a few people on board to care for the boat; in the morning we'll decide what is to be done to free ourselves from this predicament. I'm informed that there are press people at the dock. I say, "I'll go out first and speak to the press, explaining that there's some kind of engine problem." Ken takes us to the dock in the rubber boat.

There are no Greek journalists, only Yvonne Ridley and Aki Nawaz of Press TV, who will be boarding our boat here. They are more like embedded reporters, who will be with us for the ride to Cyprus and then Gaza. In that way they are not really an outside journalist and cameraman. No press statement is needed.

My wife waits for me at the pier. She has traveled 170 miles, along with other comrades to meet me here. They look mightily disappointed, although they're smiling to encourage us. Police appear and ask for the foreigners' passports. I don't give them a chance; they only get the passports of the people who disembark on the first trip of the Zodiac. Ken ferries the rest directly to shore. They haven't caught on yet to "what the beef is" with the boat; they just act like good bureaucrats.

After taking our foreign friends to Rosa Nera, the hostel where the boat passengers would be staying while in Chania, I speak with my wife and my comrades for a while, and then return to the boat and straight to bed. I was really shattered. We have succeeded in overcoming so many difficulties; we've managed to move from Eretria only to become shipwrecked in shallow water in the first harbor where we've tried to dock.

August 10

I woke up at a few minutes before seven, and the first thing I see when I get to the dock is the gargantuan figure of Markos smiling at me on the pier. He tells me later that my grumpy look then turned into a grin. When we informed Vangelis about the boat's plight, he asked Markos to come to our aid. Ken brings him to our stranded ship in the rubber boat. They both put on swimsuits, scuba tanks, and masks and then they dive. For ten minutes I watch the two divers below the surface as they search the boat thoroughly. The outcome is pretty encouraging: no damage to the boat—not even a scratch. It is sitting gently on the sandbar and didn't hit any rocks. We only have to wait for the tide.

We return ashore with Markos to get a boat that can pull us off the sandbar. The locals are absolutely certain about one thing—there is no tide here. Markos proves to be a scholar, though. He has done his own research and knows that there will be a tide of just under two inches, which is quite sufficient to get us moving. He even knows the exact time of the tide.

A bit later we experience a magnificent view: Markos and Ken dive again, place their shoulders under the boat and push. The tide is in, and there it is: our boat is moving freely again. Spyros is a local man who has a rubber boat with a strong engine. He tied up to our vessel and is now pulling us toward the dock. There is not even a sign of the slightest current. Greek seamanship has done it again. We landlubbers could not have even thought of managing such a situation. How to steer a heavy fishing boat with no engine was a really perplexing issue for us. The solution sounded quite incredible: Spyros would pull from the front, and Marcos and Ken would push from the right and left side of the stern using our own small rubber boat to help to get our bigger fishing boat off the sandbar and back on course! The boat was safely docked, and the batteries charged.

Early in the afternoon Vangelis informed us they would arrive on *Free Gaza*. They, too, had the same problem: a lack of captains with the right kind of experience to manage the heavy boat. A friend of Vangelis, who had captained tankers, began by taking the wheel to leave the harbor, and immediately chaos ensued as the boat went left when it should have gone right.

Puzzled, our Irish first mate, Derek took over, with the same result, and then the problem became clear—the ship's wheel had been installed backwards, resulting in the boat doing exactly the opposite of what it's supposed to when you steer!

The crowded Spetses harbor resounded with verbal abuse from fishermen and luxury boat owners. Once he grasped what had happened, Derek actually managed to safely steer the boat out of the harbor, and they set off to meet us even though the wheel was not working properly, had been installed backwards and was barely steerable.

When the boat reaches the outer harbor, Ken carried Markos back in the rubber boat, then piloted and moored it next to ours. Now, for the first time, the two Free Gaza movement boats are next to each other in the main harbor, the very heart of the tourist district of Chania. Banners openly proclaim our mission to the world. Our boats are now labeled with their symbolic names in English and Arabic: *SS/Free Gaza* and SS/*Liberty* [Ghaza Huriya wa Al Huriya].

On this same night, Vangelis, Paul, Derek, Markos, and I have a meeting. We decide that it is urgent to find two experienced captains for our two boats. It would be detrimental to our mission to continue with our current inexperienced captains. First thing tomorrow morning, we will look for our captains. That might prove difficult, because August is high season and everyone has gone on vacation.

Israel is now trying everything they can to stop us. Frantically, they sent out the following advisory just for our two small boats, scribbled on a piece of paper.

Advisory Notice, Maritime Zone Off The Coast Of Gaza Strip, August 11

The Israeli Navy is operating in the maritime zone off the coast of the Gaza Strip. In light of the security situation, all foreign vessels are advised to remain clear of area A in the attached map, bound by the following coordinates:

E	N
1. 34.19.02	31.46.08
2. 33.56.44	31.33.48
3. 34.29.28	31.35.42
4. 34.13.06	31.19.23

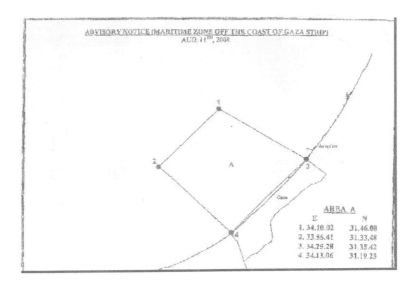

ADVISORY NOTICE (MARITIME ZONE OFF THE COAST OF GAZA STRIP)
AUG. 11TH, 2008

AREA A

	E	N
1.	34.10.02	31.46.08
2.	33.56.41	31.33.48
3.	34.29.28	31.35.42
4.	34.13.06	31.19.23

Delivery of humanitarian supplies to the civilian population in the Gaza Strip is permitted through the land crossings between Israel and the Gaza Strip, subject to prior coordination with the Israeli Authorities.

1. Vessels approaching the maritime zone off the coast of the Gaza Strip are requested to maintain radio contact with Israeli Naval Forces on Channel 16, and will be subject to supervision and inspection.

2. In accordance with the agreements between Israel and the Palestinian Authority, entry of foreign vessels to the maritime zone adjacent to the Gaza Strip is prohibited, due to the security situation and, in light of those agreements, foreign vessels are barred from such entry.

3. This notice is published in order to assure safe navigation and to prevent vessels from approaching areas in which their safety may be endangered due to the security situation in those areas.

Eliezer Marom, Adm.
Commander in Chief, Israeli Navy

Free Gaza's response to Admiral Marom's Strange Proclamation

Paul Larudee, August 12

The signature of Israeli Navy commander in chief Admiral Eliezer Marom appears on a very odd document. Dated August 11, 2008, it is not written on official stationery or addressed to anyone. The document declares that the Israeli Navy is operating in a maritime zone off the coast of Gaza. Was there any doubt that they have been doing so continuously since 1967?

It includes the sketch of a map and a series of coordinates (also attached) to define the zone, which includes all of Gaza coastal waters, and a major slice of international waters as well. It advises all foreign vessels to remain clear of this zone because of a "security situation" that is apparently so obvious that it requires no definition or explanation.

The only hint about the "security situation" is a reference to the delivery of humanitarian supplies to the civilian population in the Gaza Strip, which, according to the document, should be done only at the land crossings between Israel and the Gaza Strip (i.e., by Israeli permission only). Why is the Israeli Navy issuing a proclamation regarding the delivery of humanitarian aid by land?

The proclamation goes on to prescribe a set of protocols for vessels approaching the "maritime zone" and to prohibit vessels from entering Gaza because of the undefined "security situation."

Finally, the document pronounces its benevolent intentions to ensure "safe navigation" and its neighborly undertaking to prevent vessels from approaching an area where their safety may be endangered. Endangered? By whom? By what?

There is, of course, an explanation for such a strange document, disseminated (as nearly as can be determined) to a narrow circle of maritime authorities (we received this document from the Cypriot port authorities through our agent in Cyprus). It is that the document itself is an embarrassment to Israel, which nevertheless feels compelled to issue it in some form, as a disclaimer for any forceful action that they might take against an unnamed threat.

The embarrassment is that the unnamed threat consists of the two converted fishing boats of the Free Gaza movement, bought and refurbished in Greece, and flying Greek flags. On board is a contingent of forty-four crew, journalists and human rights advocates, sworn to nonviolence, as well as a modest cargo of hearing aids for Palestinian children in Gaza. Among our ranks are a Greek member of parliament, an eighty-one-year-old Catholic nun, and the sister-in-law of former British Prime Minister Tony Blair. No wonder Israel is embarrassed. Does Israel seriously consider the delivery of humanitarian aid to be a security crisis? Does the initiative of a small group of harmless people constitute such a threat? If so, what does that say about the kind of state to which Israelis pledge allegiance?

Finally, the declaration's kind words of interest for the safety of vessels traveling in the area hide their threat to use force against the motley flotilla that dares to challenge the entrapment of 1.5 million people in what has become the largest and most permanent concentration camp in the world, and to animate a civil rights movement where others see only a manufactured humanitarian crisis.

Israel's blockade of the Gaza coast is an affront to all peoples, but most especially the seafaring peoples of the Mediterranean, where people have lived, prospered and built great civilizations through access to the sea since time immemorial, not least in Gaza itself. To deny Palestinians this resource is a human rights obscenity that Greeks, Italians, North Africans, Turks and other seafaring peoples must unite to condemn.

Admiral Marom's proclamation shows nothing so much as the desperation and paranoia of a regime that lacks the imagination and courage to embrace a project that harms no one and delivers hope as its primary cargo. It behooves Israel to welcome the Free Gaza initiative as a step toward mutual respect for the human rights of all persons who call the land of Palestine their home.

Petros, on the *Liberty* in Crete, August 11

At about noon Markos has found us a captain. He is from Crete and in three hours time, he joins us. Giorgos Klontzas is, as of today, the main captain for FG. He comes from my wife's city, Agios Nikolaos, here on the island of Crete. It is also coincidentally, the Greek name of our boat. I have never met him. But when Markos introduces us and we have a cup of coffee together, my first positive impression turns into lasting admiration and enthusiasm.

At thirty-eight, Giorgos has lived on the sea. For years he has worked as a diver and coral fisher. This is a job way more dangerous than sponge fishing, since corals are often found at 130 meters of depth. He now has his own diving ship (one like Agios Nikolaos) and has participated in many missions such as archaeological research, wreck salvage, etc.). What really counts is the fact that he is straightforward. No ifs, ands, or buts. He is being informed about the mission and the probable danger.

He says, "I'll take you to Cyprus, and if I kind of like you, I'll take you down there [to Gaza], too" His criterion was not based on danger resulting from the Zionists, but on the mentality of his shipmates. Later I realized he isn't interested in polite behavior but the willingness to deal with life on a boat. I then remembered F. Engels' words concerning some Bakunin followers: "Would these gentlemen go with traveling on a boat on which no one would obey the captain's orders and everyone would act according to their own will?"

Vangelis and Giorgos shake hands. No contracts, no paperwork. Between two honest men, one's word and shaking hands is quite enough. Giorgos gets down to business immediately. The first thing he does is dive and search every inch of the boat's hull.

It's not that he doesn't trust his friend Markos; he wants to shape his own opinion. When I ask him why he would do that, he answers earnestly, "In my lifetime I've been through tough shit, and I know what matters are details." The first detail I could make out was that he pushes in three knife blades at three different spots of the ship.

A knife is an important tool for a small boat sailor, since in the case of an emergency he may need to cut the ropes; therefore, he always needs to have a knife handy. He and Markos start checking the engine, the bridge and the deck, while I make notes of what should be purchased and brought aboard for the necessary repairs.

Meanwhile, Derek informs us that Matthew, a second captain from the UK and living in Cyprus, is on his way.

August 12

Our new British captain and I do not share the same sentiments. But I don't pay too much attention to his personality since he is supposed to do his job as a captain, not make friends with me. From the beginning, there is conflict between Matthew and us Greeks: differences in opinion and style, which lead to heated arguments during the next few days. I make sure I calm myself down, convincing myself that it's due to a different cultural mentality.

Mathew gathers the passengers on the deck and delivers a rousing speech, and they clap as if they are just going on a day trip. Giorgos, on the other hand, is very brief when speaking during our boat's meeting: "I want only one thing from you— don't think! When I say something, just do it just as I say!" It's obvious that he doesn't need us as seamen; he needs us to be passengers, who for their own safety, respect the sea and the knowledge of their boat's captain and listen to him when they need to.

Sharyn, August 12

I remember a week ago, when we were all less worn out and all our conflicting priorities hadn't driven us quite so crazy. Our so-called "quietly spoken Greek sailing contact, Vangelis," has since done a LOT of shouting, the like of which I have never seen and hope never to see again. I literally feared his heart would give out, but he's still breathing for now.

We have gotten as far as Crete, but challenges before and since have involved such minor things as winds that completely prevent us from moving, captains not working out, having to scour the world for new ones, the satellite technology for live film that might keep us all alive not working properly and, oh by the way, we are beginning to run out of money. But it's STILL all coming together and the Gaza folks just await us with even more fervor. We hope to sail today from Crete, into conditions that our experienced sailors tell us will have us all begging for a place on the land team instead of the boats when we reach Cyprus.

We've just decided to go into debt on faith. This is too important. We would prefer as many as possible of the resources (e.g., the boats and the technical stuff) to remain in the hands of Gaza human rights organizations or Palestine solidarity projects, not to be sold afterwards to repay debts, though this may have to be an option if funds don't come in since otherwise various people who drained their own bank accounts may have to go bankrupt! We are, essentially, broke.

105

Greta, University of Cyprus, August 12

We have been informed by the boat's crews and organizers, that we have run out of money for the boats. They didn't even bother to ask us if we, the passengers waiting in Cyprus, have also run out of money just to stay here. They don't really seem to care that we are now overdrawn, overtired and overextended. We may start losing passengers in the next few days if we don't get some kind of reassurance that the boats are going to actually be here in the next week. However, Mary and I wrote the following plea and put it on the website:

> Please post this appeal to your lists far and wide. Thank you. We WILL arrive in Gaza.
>
> Two years ago, about a dozen human rights activists devised a plan to sail a boat to Gaza in order to break the siege. We rejected a plan to rent a boat as impractical because a similar venture in 1988 failed when the Israelis disabled the boat before it sailed, and the three organizers were killed. Thus no boat owner would willingly risk his craft. We ultimately decided to purchase two small boats that could carry forty-four passengers, crew, and media.
>
> Each of us contributed what we could, and we also received thousands of dollars from individual supporters. We also held fund-raising events, received a few thousand dollars from small grants, and several angels helped us along the way. Each passenger has paid his/her own way to get here, and many have raised additional money through their groups, worked extra jobs, and asked family and friends to donate. The passengers also paid an additional €700 each for lodging in Cyprus and to cover the cost of supplies and food on land and sea.
>
> Through these efforts we have raised $300,000, which we thought covered our costs. But the eroding dollar-euro exchange rate seriously drained our funds. All of our planning did not anticipate this contingency.
>
> We are now in Cyprus awaiting our boats' arrival from

106

Crete. When they come in, we will fuel up (with very high-cost diesel), and stock necessary food and supplies. We hope to cast off for Gaza this weekend. We are told that thousands of Gazans will greet us on arrival.

Many people thought we'd never come this far. But here we are, and we firmly intend to set sail regardless of some recent staggering debts. Frankly, we have spent much more than we've raised; here are just a few of our recent expenses:

Two Sailor 250 Fleet Broadband systems to allow us to stay in electronic contact and to send streaming video in real time: $16,000 each, or $32,000
Repairs to make the boats seaworthy: $25,000-$30,000
Electronics, wiring, connections, satellite uplinks, SPOT Trackers to make the system work: $5,000-$8,000
Forty-four life jackets and two hand-held GPS units: $8,000
Paint & banners for the boats, and balloons & toys for Gaza children: $2,000
Diesel fuel for both boats, both ways: $15,000 to $25,000

Except for part of the diesel fuel, we have already paid these costs by running our personal credit cards to the limit, borrowing money, and asking some of the Greek crew to help. Frankly, we're tapped out. We need your help so that we sail on the Mediterranean Sea and not on a sea of debt.

Please, donate through the PayPal account on our Web site (www.freegaza.org), send a tax-deductible check to the U.S. address on the Web site, and/or send a check to the address in the UAE. Every donation, large or small, will help keep us afloat.

And, finally, thanks for your interest, support, and prayers! The Passengers and Crew on *FREE GAZA* and *LIBERTY*

More than $50,000 came in over the next few days, giving us hope and making us believe in ourselves once more.

Dicing with Death for Gaza

Yvonne Ridley, on board the Free Gaza, August 13

By the time you read this, our two boats, the *Free Gaza* and *Liberty* should be sailing from Chania's old port in Crete despite a gloomy forecast of storms ahead. Our captains have decided it is time to quit our dock for security reasons, and so we are heading along the Cretan coastline on our way to pick up the rest of our passengers who have been waiting patiently in Larnaca, Cyprus. We could be in for a rough ride, but we would probably be more at risk by not moving. Israel has a history of using Mossad to sabotage and destroy peaceful operations designed to help or show solidarity with Palestinians.

Media interest is once again gathering momentum and there are those who want to join us on board while others are considering hiring their own boats. Wouldn't it be great if we had a huge flotilla? The more the merrier. However, there are concerns from the media because Israel has a history of shooting, killing, and arresting journalists who try to report the truth about the brutal occupation of Palestine. I was reminded of this only this morning as I read a release from Reporters without Borders. The human rights group was condemning today's announcement by the IOF (Israeli Occupation Forces) to detain Ibrahim Hamad, a soundman employed by the Palestinian news agency Ramattan, for six months without bringing charges and without taking him before any court.

Israeli soldiers arrested Hamad at his home in Qalandia, near the West Bank city of Ramallah, on July 15. "The Israeli military may not under any circumstances arrest journalists or media assistants without giving a reason," Reporters without Borders said. "If they think a journalist has done something wrong, they must say what it is and they must explain why they are arresting him. We call for Hamad's immediate release."

When reached by Reporters without Borders, the management of Ramattan firmly condemned his arrest and called for his release. They also called on the Israeli authorities to explain why they are holding him. "This is not the first time that one of our employees has been arrested by the Israeli military," the agency said.

Israel boasts it is a democracy—these are not the actions of a democratic state. These are the actions of a brutal state that tries to crush those dedicated to telling the truth about the full horrors of the Zionist regime and its determination to see through its deliberate and slow genocide of the Palestinian people.

We will be able to see in a few days time exactly how the Israelis react to a group of peaceful activists who want to sail into Gaza armed with nothing more than love and support for their Palestinian brothers and sisters. If Israel is really a free and open democracy then its navy will let us pass. Mossad will stop trying to sabotage our journey and all of the journalists on board, including me, will be able to report the truth about what is happening in the world's largest open-air prison—Gaza. In the meantime, I would urge the IOF to release our brother Ibrahim Hamad and allow him to continue his media work.

Aki Nawaz, August 12

"You could be killed, so do you still want to go?"

These were the words of Yvonne Ridley as she asked me if I would be willing to be her cameraman for a historical journey to Gaza, Palestine. Yes, Palestine, a place and people that have endured a modern injustice and tragedy far beyond comprehension; we would be given a chance of exposing the condition of the powerful political class; that its values are not only repulsive but more so, shameless.

Instinctively I always knew it was in my fate to get to Palestine and what better way than one that not only tested someone, but also avoided every interaction, recognition of any illegal authority of Israel or permission via their imposed dominance in the region. "I am honored to go," was my humble response and everything was put into place with lightning speed and conviction. It was a secret from family and friends, as I wrote out a will in the event of my death.

But this journey was not only a test, or some "romantic notion" of achievement. It was a religious and spiritual journey that opened my eyes, heart and mind to the many layers of humanity and goodwill. It put into perspective that "good people" are in abundance and from many backgrounds. I knew this before, but never experienced it in its totality; there are many "unknown heroes" that never carry the notion of "self" or "our interest" as a religious edict, unlike the political ramblings of the powerful.

The camera became my teacher, as it dwelled deep into the lives of those 44 or so activists from every background imaginable: the lovers to the militant, the intellect to the spiritual, the anarchist to the fundamentalist, and more; all grouped together with the spirit and focus on breaking the "Siege of Gaza" by sea.

It had been attempted before, but the forces of injustice had undermined it and everything was against the odds. This time, the passion of experienced activists in this cause was overwhelming and inspiring. Those that had met and suffered at the hands of the IOF on previous occasions were in high spirits and we were in beautiful caring hands.

The sound bite of "plain sailing" was never so far from the truth. As we arrived in Cyprus, engaged madly with our new-found friends, all age groups and all nationalities, I pondered: "Who will live and who would die?", as we captured their spirits on camera and, in a couple of days, flew to Crete to rendezvous with our "sea angels" or ships. They would carry us to our victory; or maybe, to our death.

The honeymoon of romantic visions disappeared as reality kicked in and problem upon problem landed in our laps. The ships, the authorities and the mission itself was tested on all fronts. It was beyond patience; it was a test of will, as an envisioned 7-day journey turned into weeks of a bizarre form of democracy: no leaders, just voices all participating and worthy of opinion. Never before did I wish to be ruled and dominated as much, but this was never going to be "text book" activism; this was more special.

In the darkness of night, we began the long uncharted journey with people of spirit and adventure, travelling toward our destination; each one of us challenged in every possible way. Doing things in straight lines was never appealing to me. But was this "walking and talking backwards," or was it a wiser hand guiding us?

The narrative cannot be written, as 50 or so different films were in the making or maybe hundreds, including those that did not take the journey but blessed, donated and pushed the ships along the beautiful landscapes and water-filled horizons of the Mediterranean. The justified paranoia of "Mossad" followed us. Were they going to preemptively stop us? or maybe they were just too busy planning illegal assassinations.

We became self-destructive, as people tested their own resilience, and some literally jumped ship. The journey was far from the starting point; and as we sailed toward Cyprus, the sea was not cooling us as it should. Instead, we were riding a storm of volcanic flow. Maybe the gift of language is not always as beneficial to the human race; words, thoughts and opinions were delaying the action as a battle of tactics was in full flow.

Yvonne never said I could die from conversation and discussion, but I swear I nearly did. I did, however, learn the art of patience in its extreme.

Dr. Bill, University of Cyprus, August 13

Back home, I am usually an early-to-sleep and early-to-rise kind of guy. Here, I try to do both because the night and the early morning are the most tolerable times of the day in Cyprus in terms of temperature and we have no air conditioning in any of the rooms where we sleep, just in the room where we meet. When I can, I spend the late afternoon sleeping in my dorm room with the fan on or hiking a couple kilometers away with other FG passengers to cool off in an outdoor community swimming pool.

Twice I try jogging in the park at 6:00 A.M. One morning, Rashid joins me. He is as sleek as a greyhound, while I'm more like a tank. Fortunately, this is social jogging, and Rashid mercifully decides not to leave me in the dust. We jog at my pace and end up talking about what we might do while we are waiting for the boats to arrive.

Our boats continue to be delayed and this is frustrating; they are in Crete, where they have gone public. Now there are photographs of the *Free Gaza* and the *Liberty* out there on the World Wide Web. Lauren Booth, Huwaida Arraf, and Jeff Halper have all joined the boats in Greece, and have held a press conference with Paul Larudee, Vangelis and other organizers.

But there is also bad news, like cost overruns; we all need to dig deeper into our own pockets and give more, and those of us who can, do. To make matters worse, the boats can't cross the straits between the Greek islands and Cyprus yet; first because of equipment needs, and then high waves.

Tom Nelson, one of our lawyers and a passenger as well, is heading off to Saudi Arabia to visit a few clients while we wait. Some of our passengers are thinking of going to Lebanon for a few days. After all, Beirut is only a twenty-minute flight from Larnaca; the drive from here to the airport takes longer.

Rashid is thinking about flying to Tel Aviv and then making

his way to the West Bank, since he has never been there before. As a veteran traveler to the West Bank and Israel, and with experience passing through Ben Gurion airport more than once, I try to give him advice. The main problem is that Ben Gurion usually does not allow Muslim Arabs to pass through the airport. Rashid is from Algeria but has spent most of his life in the UK and has a British accent and a British passport.

As we jog through the park and past the waterfowl along the lake behind the reservoir, we try to decide whether he should try and use his BBC press pass.

"I know!" he says. "I can pass myself off as an Arab Jew."

"Yeah," I pant back. "You look like many Sephardic Jews I have seen in Israel. You could claim that you left Algeria for London because you were part of a persecuted minority...pant....You were raised as an agnostic Jew. Now you are coming to Israel to get in touch with your Jewish heritage...pant...pant...Once you get past customs, you can take a group taxi to Jerusalem, and I can put you in touch with contacts who work for the International Solidarity Movement. They can put you in touch with contacts in the West Bank. Once you are inside, you can do whatever you want.

Rashid is ecstatic at the prospect. We finish our jog and shower down in the dorm. We wind up in the kitchen for breakfast and explain our elaborate plan to Tom.

"It sounds interesting," he remarks. "The only problem with your plan is that your passport gives your name as Rashid. What kind of a Jewish name is that?"

Rashid decides to rethink this whole plan and ends up not flying to Tel Aviv. He winds up exploring the Turkish side of Cyprus for a few days instead. The only good part about this delay is that we get to watch some of the Beijing Olympics, which we would have missed entirely had our mission been on schedule. One person who doesn't have enough time to watch much of the Olympics is Greta Berlin. One of the main original organizers, Greta is now head of the media team. Like

Osama, Paul and Sharyn back in Greece, she is becoming exhausted from not getting enough sleep. Her phone is ringing incessantly; and she still receives anonymous death threats that unsettle the nerves.

Her dorm room is like Grand Central Station, since she has one of the few laptops that is hooked up to the Internet. The college campus technicians who arrange Internet hookup here at the university are all on their August vacation, so late arrivals like me are stuck. Greta tries to take fitful naps in her dorm room while others are taking turns at her desk working off her laptop at all hours of the night and day checking their e-mail accounts.

Greta, along with Hedy and others, is doing multiple press conferences and radio interviews every day and arranging other interviews for the rest of us. The temperature is over 40 degrees C, (over 100 degrees F), and there is no air conditioning. She is in an awkward spot in terms of maintaining her credibility with the media because the world press wants accurate, specific information about when the Free Gaza movement boats will be leaving Cyprus for Gaza. But this is precisely the kind of information that must be kept fuzzy for a variety of logistical and security reasons.

Hedy Epstein is also working overtime with wall-to-wall press interviews, keeping up a very hectic pace for an almost eighty-four-year-old woman. I don't think she is getting enough rest. But as a holocaust survivor who worked at the Nürnberg trials, with longstanding public record promoting human rights, she is an obvious media focus for our campaign.

Mary Hughes has been burning the midnight oil working as the chief financial officer, caught in the middle of the current financial crisis of the Free Gaza movement. She has been at her laptop for hours helping Greta write urgent appeals for financial help and circulating them far and wide. Amazingly, the appeal put out by the Free Gaza movement just a few days ago has generated almost $50,000 in the PayPal account, plus a benefactor in the Bay Area has offered to loan us $100,000, knowing that he may never get it back. We are going to be OK... unless there are more delays.

Petros, aboard *Agios Nikolaos* somewhere along the north coast of Crete, August 13

Today we really need to get going. No reason for any further delay. There's been a very good press conference at the pier right in front of the two boats, which turned into a political solidarity event, in which dozens of progressive people from Chania, as well as many Arab immigrants, participated. The boats are ready.

The captains are both professional. And the most important reason for moving now is that we've been informed that the Greek Foreign Ministry, which doesn't hesitate to show its pro-American, pro-Israeli face, has intervened with the Ministry of Maritime Affairs, asking it to sabotage our journey.

It can use a very simple way: a technical check of the boats can keep us in Limbo in Chania for up to two weeks, meaning that the already delayed mission will get way out of schedule. That would increase the chance of it being canceled or weakened to such a degree that the Zionists could stop us somewhere between Cyprus and Gaza.

The weather seems to be an obstacle to our cause, too. At this time of the year, the westerly and northwesterly winds blow. The forecast shows increasing gale force winds in the southern Aegean for the next few days. Giorgos, Markos, and Vangelis, who also have maritime experience, believe that we really have to leave Chania just in case a problem of check and delay comes up. We are at the western end of Crete, and we must reach the eastern end where we then turn on a southeastern heading toward Cyprus. Why waste time then? Let's travel along the northern Cretan coast all the way to Sitia

115

(the far eastern city of Crete). There, we can reconsider the weather and, when given the chance, we can sail to Cyprus. Yes, we can.

Mathew looks hesitant, avoiding a direct expression of his opinion. He talks about harsh weather, but, mind you, it's only a wind level of four on the Beaufort scale (seven, we would have to worry about). This sounds silly to me. We need to get going, even if means a few rough seas. This is not a pleasure cruise that we are going on. It is a holy mission to be accomplished. He has to agree, so it's late at night, and we are leaving Chania.

Vangelis has looked after the sail permit; we have told authorities we are heading to Rhodes. In this way, the ministry people will go there and won't be able to stop us. We have secretly decided not to sail to Rhodes at all.

Let the bureaucrats and inspectors who want to tie us up in red tape wait for us there. I deliberately misinform our people in Sitia that we have changed our mind and will go to Rhodes after all. If my phone has been bugged (which is quite certainly the case), the bureaucratic inspectors will get the wrong information, allowing us to keep moving out into international waters toward Cyprus.

August 14

I wake up at 6:00 A.M. and go to the bridge to find out if Giorgos wants me to steer. He is outraged. "I'm looking for *Free Gaza* and can't see it anywhere. We specifically told Matthew to be right behind us, and he's just disappeared!" The weather goes swimmingly, only two to three on the Beaufort scale.

I call Vangelis aboard on his mobile and wake him up. "We've lost you!" Giorgos gives him our position and describes it according to the nearest bearings on the Cretan coast. Vangelis calls me back; he is really pissed. Matthew has led them to Iraklion. Vangelis asked him to continue on the same route behind us and he replied, "You can steer if you like."

Well, now we have to make a stop at Iraklion; at first we're in the middle of the harbor and then at a remote dock. At our meeting, tension between us is mounting. The issue is partly a cultural one. Some of the British and Americans who have some sailing experience have more confidence in Matthew's views and Giorgos' local experience inspires the Greeks and other passengers with more confidence. Matthew probably thinks we are all crazy anyway.

What we have here is a failure to communicate. Ships such as ours have been traveling in a lot worse weather all round the Mediterranean. Rarely have they ever overturned or sunk. Greek sponge divers and fishermen reached Gibraltar many a time paddling small boats.

Paul is cool, calm and diplomatic with the idea of continuing on. "We've got Captain Giorgos with us, and he is also very experienced in these waters. Who will not take his advice?" I, on the other hand, am furious. I plead to our friends to trust the Greeks; after all, they know this sea thoroughly. Giorgos can give you the position of every single island, even of every rock and small reef. Our boats are not yachts, but they are sturdy. They still rock and pitch a lot and with the smallest of waves. We'll have a hard trip; that's for sure, especially further south, where the sea gets rougher. But, these are safe vessels.

Don't forget, they're expecting us in Cyprus. Don't forget our mission. We think the boat passengers who are frightened should fly to Cyprus and then those who remain can sail the boats to Cyprus in peace.

August 15

Having wasted a whole day, we aboard the *Liberty* decide to leave at noon. It's quite simple, we'll just push on; the other boat will have to follow us. We inform them of our intentions. At about 6:00 P.M., we reach Sitia. Just before we enter the harbor, I call our friends to say we are about to arrive in their port in Sitia. I'd deliberately misled them—and anyone bugging the phone—about our itinerary. They are mighty surprised. Today is one of the three greatest festivals in Greece. Our local friends, Theodosius and Dimitris, join us within a few minutes of our arrival. More people come as night falls. Having made a list that settles the night watch duty shifts, we gather at a café to have the much-needed shots of raki.

August 16

At noon, lots of our friends from Sitia come to the boat, bringing us fruit and food. They have invited the local media, and we organise a new press conference. In the afternoon *Free Gaza* finally arrives and now Ken is the captain, even though he is not qualified to sail a boat of this size.

Matthew just left them and went back to Cyprus. I'm at the pier with Giorgos, who watches every detail, encouraging Ken through his docking procedure, a partially lit cigarette butt hanging from his mouth. "Good job, Ken! That's the stuff!" He is the first to shake hands with Ken as he steps onto the pier. Giorgos' teamwork makes me regard him with even higher esteem!

We have decided to get us a second captain who holds a Greek license to sail *Free Gaza* to Larnaka. After that we'll see what to do. Giorgos has called an acquaintance of his, who will soon join us after settling some personal business.

During the night, as Yiannis and I take a stroll down the waterfront of this little harbor, we come across Giorgos. He wants to buy us a drink. We make small talk for quite a while. I'm really impressed by his stories. "Last year I went to Kalymnos to attend a local diving festival. When I saw the sponge divers dancing their dance, I was really touched, and wept. Everybody else applauded, but I wept." What did Giorgos know? Kalymnos is the island of the sponge divers. Quite a few of them are struck by the bends and end up crippled. Their dance involves the first dancer pretending to be a crippled sponge diver who's trying to get up and dance, bending on a walking stick.

There's one more thing that Giorgos tells me and impresses on me. "I've been through lots of difficulties, and I learned not to allow myself to get desperate."

Donna Wallach – August 17

We have been waiting in Cyprus for two weeks for the *Free Gaza* and the *Liberty* to arrive, to join the others already onboard, so we can set sail to Gaza, Palestine, to break the deadly Israeli siege. In frustration, we are making banners, trying to not get in each other's way and do something constructive. So, I sat down and wrote this background piece last night.

All of Israel, East Jerusalem, the West Bank and the Gaza Strip is Occupied Palestine. The Israeli Occupation has been continuing without let-up and expanding since 1948. The Gaza Strip, located along the coast at the southern end of Palestine, has been occupied by Israel since 1967. The apartheid Israeli government has not allowed the Gaza Strip to develop economically. The Gazans are restricted as to what kind of businesses they can open, who they can trade with internationally and what products they can make – they are not permitted to have any business which would compete with Israeli markets.

Since 2006, the Gaza Strip has been under an Israeli

genocidal siege. Israel closed all the border crossings, not letting people or supplies in or out. Even very sick people who urgently need medical care in hospitals inside Israel or in Egypt are not permitted to leave the Gaza Strip. By 2008, over 215 Palestinians have died because they were refused permission to receive the medical care that would have saved their lives. Scores of children have been among those who have died.

In the Gaza Strip, 10 percent of the children suffer from malnutrition, stunting their growth and development. Eighty percent of the population is totally dependent on UNRWA for their food. According to the United Nations Office for the Coordination of Humanitarian Affairs, "Most U.N. food assistance only makes up a portion of the daily needs."

Gaza has fertile land where crops used to grow; however, Israeli soldiers have repeatedly destroyed the crops and the irrigation pipes, depriving the Palestinians of their livelihood and the ability to feed their families.

Their drinking water has also been affected. In December 2007, due to lack of necessary spare parts for the regular repair and maintenance of the water network, "three wells in Gaza City were unable to operate at their full potential, leaving 140,000 people with access to water for only 4-6 hours per day." In the summer, temperatures in Gaza are in the 100s Fahrenheit (40 Celsius). Water treatment projects in various cities in the Gaza Strip are on hold because Apartheid Israel won't permit the necessary equipment to be imported.

Gazan students who have graduated from high school and want to attend university can't continue their studies in the universities inside the West Bank. Those students with scholarships, even Fulbright scholarships, are denied the necessary visas by Israel to leave the Gaza Strip to go to their destined campuses worldwide.

All of us in the Free Gaza movement, whether passengers on the boats or part of the support teams, are outraged that 1.5 million Palestinians are being collectively punished by the apartheid policies of the Israeli state. The governments of the world and international organizations have the power to force Israel to open the borders to allow the Palestinians to travel in and out of Gaza, and the West Bank, too; to allow the transport of food, medicine, school books, fuel and replacement parts for machinery and hospital equipment. They are standing by and watching this collective punishment continue unabated.

This deadly siege on Gaza Strip is 21st century slow-motion genocide. The Palestinian people are being slowly but surely killed, their culture destroyed and their families torn apart. The entire world is watching while this happens; it has been watching this happen for over 60 years. The Free Gaza movement says NO! We are starting by breaking this illegal siege – it has to end, we demand that it end now. We are sailing on two boats to break this deadly siege.

Please join us, tell everyone you know that the Israeli siege of Gaza must end! There now, I feel a bit better.

Dr. Bill, August 18

Now we are hearing that our boats are only a couple days away from Larnaca Port, and our excitement grows. Derek Graham is sent to talk to those of us still waiting in Nicosia and to brief us about security issues. He is an Irish electrician living in Limassol, Cyprus and also has seamanship skills. He is also streetwise about Cyprus. He has been with the boats and is here to urge caution as we enter another vulnerable period.

"Look," Derek explains. "Cyprus is famous for two things: its prostitutes and its spies."

"With Greeks, Turks, Russians, Armenians, Israelis, Arabs, Brits, Americans, and others passing in and out of here, there is espionage from every direction. Be very careful. The last thing we need now is to have one of us 'disappeared.' No one should go anywhere alone. Travel in pairs or in multiples. Avoid hassles and walk away from large crowds. We don't need someone shot or stabbed in a large crowd by some unknown assailant."

"Stop using cell phones when you get to Larnaca. Israeli mobile phone technology is among the most advanced in the world. They can use GPS to pinpoint your location. Use calling cards and local pay phones instead. Those are more anonymous. Use new and different SIM cards to create secure networks of friends. Call only other secure phones with fresh SIM cards from within your select network of friends who also have new secure SIM cards, which have never been used to call other phone numbers outside your small network. Otherwise your new number is no longer secure."

"When we get to the boats, we will maintain close watch, with a land-based person, and a boat person who has previously traveled with the boats from Greece. We will provide continuous night watch for each boat at all times."

Some of us were planning to attend a music festival in Plakos, Cyprus, during the final weekend before leaving. We have already bought our tickets. But in consideration of what we have heard from Derek, we reluctantly decide that we better stay put at the university. A mosh pit at some music festival is probably not the best place to be hanging out right now because we have little control over what could happen in that situation.

Petros: Across the Carpathian Sea, August 17

Captain Zacharias is an able seaman who's worked on merchant ships for years. He arrives in the morning and, after a short conversation with Vangelis, agrees to pilot *Free Gaza* all the way to Larnaka. He also talks with Giorgos and they decide we should not go straight to Cyprus, but follow a course near the islands, even if that means wasting half a day. We will be crash testing the boats in the open sea and need to be off the coast in case any serious damage develops.

At 10:30, we sail, and we are lucky. The Carpathian, the roughest Greek sea, is absolutely calm. Not a wave to worry about. On the VHF, we hear people on ships sailing nearby: "Never seen this sea so calm in my life" says a captain. Giorgos catches a tuna around 7 kilos. He pulls it up slowly and everybody applauds as he brings it on the deck. What about cooking it, then? We've got gas but no cooking utensils!

Vangelis suggests that we have it raw. Sushi time! He undertakes the task to cut off some pieces around the fish's head. We dip them in lemon and, in a few minutes, yummy sushi is ready to be served. I've never tasted such a delicacy in all my life!

As the daylight wanes, our ships smoothly sail on a really calm sea. The sun goes down behind the mountains of Karpathos. An amazing wonderful view! Then, the full moon of August rises, reflecting its gold on the seawater.

Giorgos and Nikos do not share these moments of peace. There's been an oil leak. They repair the damage temporarily until we reach land and fix it properly.

August 18

I wake up early in the morning at sea only to see *Free Gaza* tied behind our boat. Their engine is shut off, and we are towing them. What happened? There's been a problem with steering, and so we tow them in order to avoid further delay until Captain Zacharias and Ken fix the damage. After the repair, we untie the boat, and we all sail on while remaining in visual contact.

A short while before noon, we reach Kastelorizo, the last Greek island, next to the Turkish coast. Takis and Yiannis recollect that they have an old mate, Andreas, from university, who lives on the island. They get in touch with him and brief him. While getting closer to the island, a rubber boat with Andreas and the mayor of the island approaches us. They escort us to the center of the small harbor, where the mayor receives us warmly and makes arrangements for a lunch for all of us.

The people of Kastelorizo have their own historical bonds with Gaza. During the Second World War, the island was under Italian occupation. The British wanted to bomb it, so all its inhabitants had to leave and take refuge in Gaza. The mayor's maternal aunt was born in Gaza. And now two Greek boats are paying their last Greek port of call to their island. They are part of an international mission to sail on to Gaza to break the siege.

It is night and our captains discuss the issue of our departure as the forecast doesn't sound too good. Giorgos suggests we leave in the morning. Zacharias insists we leave immediately. The locals tell us that bad weather doesn't last long. Then, both captains agree.

We set sail an hour before midnight. Two rubber boats escort us to the open sea. Heading to the south, the weather is fine again. Not even a breeze. Only the swell, the silent wave of the Mediterranean Sea, makes its presence clear. We have gotten used to it by now.

Greta, Cyprus, August 17

Paul called and said we have no captain for the *Free Gaza*. The English captain refused to work with the Greeks after several big arguments. He insisted that the boats were not safe, and he was not going to pilot what looked like a shipwreck. Our first mate, Derek, agrees that the two fishing boats are barely seaworthy, but, by now, we have invested over $500,000 in both of them. Derek tells us we could have bought a yacht in Cyprus for what we paid for the two decrepit boats we are now trying to sail.

The steering wheel on one was installed backwards; the fan belt on the other breaks all of the time, the boats weave and shift in the water at the slightest wave movement, we should have a boat engineer on both just to keep the engines going, and still the Greeks say they are shipshape and can take the passengers without worrying.

We're stuck. We're going to take them no matter what, but I do tell the passengers what the situation is in case they decide not to come. So far, we have only lost four people, mostly because their schedules simply won't permit them to stay any longer. Surprisingly, we still have 44 crazy passengers.

At one of our last meetings in Nicosia, I ask if anyone knows a captain who could be ready for sailing in 4-5 days. Kathy Sheetz, our emergency room nurse, pipes up and says, "I'll call my brother, John. He's used to captaining massive research ships. Maybe he will come."

And damned if he didn't say, "Yes! Send me a ticket and I can get there right away." He was on the next flight out of California. We now had a captain with more experience than anyone on large boats except for Giorgos.

Dr. Bill, Cyprus, August 19

This afternoon, we are hosted at the high-rise apartment of Nora, a Palestinian living in Cyprus, who grew up in Beirut, Lebanon. We are each given the book, *Life at the Crossroads: a History of Gaza,* by British author Gerald Butt. The view from Nora's apartment is breathtaking. We can see all of Nicosia, both the Greek and Turkish sides, and far off into the countryside. We are interviewed by Greek Cypriot television.

The next day, people on the street are starting to recognize us, saying they have seen us on TV. My attempts at acquiring medical supplies for the boats have not produced many results yet. As time gets short, it calls for more desperate measures. I appeal to my fellow passengers to pool the pharmaceuticals we

125

have for the general good. I spend the final mornings with Sr. Anne Montgomery inventorying our stock, and afternoons at a downtown Nicosia pharmacy purchasing the stocks of bandages, bedpans, and other supplies that we don't have, at my own expense. Sharyn also donated a medical kit that is quite helpful, but it is not enough.

I spend the final afternoon before we leave for Larnaca Port with Kathy Sheetz, the retired ICU nurse, organizing our medical stockpiles for each ship.

Her brother John arrived yesterday, an able sea captain who flew here from the Bay Area of California to pilot the *Free Gaza*. John is tense, wanting to get down to the boat, and I am tense, trying to work with his sister to finalize the medical inventory. It's getting time to cast our fate to the wind. Our dreams of sailing to Gaza to break the siege are becoming real.

Sister Anne, Hedy, Lynn and Tom are on the way to class... again, with our "Gaza on my Mind" T-shirts.

126

Chapter 6: The Spies Who Didn't Love Us

Petros Giotis, Bill Dienst, Greta Berlin, Mary Hughes Thompson, Sharyn Lock,

Petros, Aboard *Liberty*, August 19

It's morning. Everybody wakes up. The weather is still fine, and we travel smoothly to Cyprus. A little later, one of the side protective balloon fenders falls into the sea. Captain Giorgos doesn't share our disappointment. He idles the engine, dives into the sea and recovers the balloon. Everybody claps.

Late at night, we approach the city lights of Pafos. The Cypriot Coast Guard calls us through the ship's radio that we must shut off all the boat lights, so they can escort us in under cover. It's obvious that they are worried about our safety. (Each boat could become the target of Zionist commandos).

August 20

We reach Larnaka at eight in the morning. We are asked to head to the guarded harbor, not the small marina. We are received as VIPs by the harbor authorities. They assure us they will be at our disposal at any time. An armed sentry is positioned by our boats. Two Cypriot Coast Guard divers search thoroughly under the boats, and there's an underwater camera installed, which is connected with a van on the pier.

Captain Giorgos has now committed himself to joining us all the way to Gaza as a member of the mission. He has caught the Gaza fever bug just like all the rest of us.

This impossible dream now seems like it could actually come to fruition. The *Free Gaza* and *Liberty* are in Larnaca Port now under Cypriot Coast Guard protection. It looks like we could get out to sea toward Gaza; but we are still not sure we can actually get in. The Israeli government has made several proclamations to the effect that they will intercept our boats and not let us pass into Gaza.

For the past few weeks, both the Greek and Cypriot governments have been under intense pressure at the highest levels from Israeli government officials and their diplomats, who are trying to stop us. Greece and Cyprus have stood firm with the majority of their citizens who support Palestinian civil rights. "They haven't any laws," they say to Israeli officials. We have to be certain that this remains the case.

We must move our supplies from the University of Cyprus to the Port of Larnaca in stages because we have limited car space. Our baggage is first piled up high behind locked doors within our dorms so we can keep an eye on it. When volunteers from Nicosia offer their cars, the luggage is brought to the curb. We each take turns providing continuous watch of our bags near the curb. The last thing we need right now is to have some Mossad agent posing as a college student walking past our bags and slipping drugs, weapons or other contraband inside our suitcases. This could then be discovered by Cypriot Coast Guard authorities who are charged with assuring safety and clearing of customs, and really mess up our operation. We cram the entire luggage as tight as we can into the first group of cars, and the first group of passengers departs for the port. We in the second group are detailed to do cleanup.

We cruise in Renee's rental car along Cypriot superhighways. Renee has already figured out how not to get lost on previous trips between Nicosia and Larnaca. So this voyage is very quick, and I am content to sit back and listen to the compilation of theme songs we have created for the voyage playing on the rental car's CD player.

We are all dropped off at a hotel that Renee arranged, which is located within walking distance to the boats. We are late to a mandatory meeting of all FG passengers. We enter an overcrowded hotel room to reunite with our colleagues who have been on the boats from Greece. They are tired; some have recently enjoyed their first showers in over a week. They need a couple more days on shore before we are ready to set sail for Gaza.

When we leave the hotel, a hippie dude and his girlfriend try to follow us everywhere we go. Fortunately, these hippies have not yet figured out a way to get into the guarded port. As far as the hotel goes, all they or their associates have to do is just walk in. I am told that this duo was in Crete with our boats and have followed us here. He is barefoot, has blond dreadlocks and speaks English with an eastern European accent. She is a brunette who dresses more like a conventional summer tourist.

They push around a shopping cart full of their belongings. They look like they would fit in well among the homeless who inhabit warm water ports around the world. I can't see it, but I'll bet that hidden in their junk within the depths of their shopping cart is a sophisticated spy camera. Maybe we are being bugged as well! In their presence, we all revert back to speaking in code words.

One morning, several of us are outside the port gate at a coffee shop. We are all waiting with our passports for clearance by Cypriot port authorities to get our credentials so we can enter and leave the guarded portion of the port. The hippie couple is right there amongst us. The surreal begins to become normal.

Paul Larudee walks right up to the man, says "Good Morning," and shakes hands with him. The whole scene becomes quite comical. We caution each other to be careful what we say or even make up things. After all, it's worked for us so far, as Israel was convinced our boats were in Egypt rather than Greece.

It could be that the hippies are the diversion, and the more normal looking group of Greek Cypriot men sitting right behind us might be the real spies. In fact, that is the most likely scenario. These two are way too conspicuous.

With our credentials we can now pass through the checkpoint that gets us inside the secure area of Larnaca port. Huge cargo ships are being loaded and unloaded on the dock toward the shore from our boats. The *Liberty* and *Free Gaza* are docked adjacent to each other in their entire splendor with flags from various nations flying aloft. There are armed Cypriot Coast Guard security men milling about. All night long, we keep a minimum of two of our own passengers aboard each ship standing guard in two-hour shifts to watch for any unusual events. Scuba divers check the bottoms of each of our boats periodically to assure they are safe.

Greta, August 20

When the boats finally appeared on the horizon of Larnaca, we were overjoyed. We really did have boats. The problem was that we didn't have two captains. The *Liberty* was going to be OK, but the *Free Gaza* was 'captainless'. We didn't dare push the rules by letting Nikos, Ken or Vittorio captain the boat, even though they probably could. But we wouldn't be allowed out of the Cypriot port, and we certainly didn't want to risk being stopped by the Israeli Navy and asked for papers. We were going to go by the book on captains.

Kathy Sheetz said her brother might be able to come at the last minute, because he was nursing a foot injury and couldn't go back to his regular captain job on the research vessel. Sharyn and I decided hiring a captain with a foot injury would be better than having no captain, so we bought John a ticket with the last of our money, and he was due to show up the day before we left.

Ken was furious and didn't understand that our decision to hire John was not only practical, it was a maritime necessity. After spending a couple of hours cooling him down, he grudgingly agreed that we might have a point. He didn't have a pilot's license for the size boat we were taking; the Greeks had already verified that. So we were now sailing with one furious ex-captain and one captain with a cast on his leg. No wonder Sharyn was ready to pack it all in and say she wasn't going. Again, our individual egos got in the way of the collective desire to sail to Gaza. It wouldn't be the first time and it definitely was not the last.

Nikos was mad at Osama, Osama was mad at Sharyn, everyone was mad at Ken, and the passengers who had stayed so patiently in Cyprus just wanted to get the hell on the boats and leave. We also had a boat crew versus land crew friction. We were upset with them, because it had taken so long to get to Cyprus; they were upset with us, because we didn't understand how difficult it had been. So, we might have the boats, but were we going to stick together?

Mary, August 21

The boats finally arrived and we have gone down to see them. They looked so tiny moored next to these huge cargo ships, but the authorities in Cyprus weren't taking any chances and wanted us to be in the international docking area rather than the marina.

We didn't realize that we actually had to go through passport control to go to Gaza. We just figured we'd get on a boat and sail off to the territory. After all, it was only 240 miles away. But Cyprus is now in the EU and has to follow the EU maritime regulations. We were leaving the EU to a foreign port, and just like at an airport, we had to show our passports

131

and get them stamped.

I don't know if we were more shocked at the tininess of the boats or the fact that we were really going to go.

Sharyn, decompressing in Larnaca, August 21

I can't say much more because the Internet man is about to throw us out. I am so tired and just rang my good friend to cry at him for a while about various internal group difficulties I might once have had the capacity to fix but don't any more. Coupled with this decreased ability to solve conflicts is an increased capacity to empathize beyond any reasonable amount with what everyone in the conflict is feeling and to feel very compassionate for individuals, while simultaneously feeling alienated with people generally. Argh!

Our boats are covered with flags and they look beautiful. Not being a flag type person, I never thought to bring the Aboriginal flag I was given last time I was in Oz (Australia), which I feel sad about. On the other hand, the Port Authorities don't seem to like any flags they don't recognize.

We had a press link with Gaza today, and they are thrilled we are finally coming. They have been waiting such a long time for us. We could learn patience from them. Israeli prison would be a pleasant rest after all this work and stress, but we have friends waiting for us.

Petros, August 21

At 13:30, there's a press conference and a ceremony for fourteen murdered Palestinian fishermen. Greek MP, Tasos Kourakis is in Cyprus with a parliamentary delegation. Takis contacts him. He visits the boats, asks to join us and he is joyously received, thus reinforcing the mission.

Meanwhile, two 'alleged' Mossad agents are pretending to be hippies. They have been stalking us from Athens and at every Cretan port where we have stopped, there they are. Now they appear in Larnaka. They can't get in the port, since security measures are tough, but they move around the hotel where members of our mission are staying and at an Internet café. Takis Politis is pissed and launches verbal abuse at them but they remain calm.

Dr. Bill, August 21

On the final afternoon and evening before departure, we hold press conferences on the dock next to the boats. We hold memorials (with international cameras rolling) for fourteen Gaza fishermen, who have been murdered since 2005 by the Israeli Navy. We also hold a memorial for thirty-four American sailors of the *USS Liberty* who were killed by the Israeli Air Force just off the Gaza Coast during the Six Day War in 1967, their deaths ignored by the world.

At the last minute, Greta wanted to know if we could find four-dozen red roses to throw into the sea, as each person's name was read aloud. Where were we going to find four-dozen red roses two hours before the press conference? A half-hour before we began, there was Renee, her arms filled with red roses. Once again, she came to our rescue and found roses, which we ceremoniously tossed into the harbor.

We do our best to command the world's attention, hoping that this will raise world awareness and also protect us. Each of the boats is equipped with camera crews, satellite phones, and news agencies like the Palestinian Ramattan, which are capable of real-time streaming television coverage on the Internet. Our story is now being broadcast to networks around the world.

I spend the final half hour before midnight with many of my shipmates inside the Internet café alongside the hotel right before closing time. I am e-mailing my friends and family to say good-bye.

133

Chapter 7: Terror, Sea Sickness and Sumud

Mary Hughes Thompson, Bill Dienst, Petros Giotis, Greta Berlin, Ren Tawil, Sharyn Lock, Aki Nawaz

> Before sailing, we were told that if any one of us was unwilling to drown at sea or be shot or arrested or dragged to Israel and thrown in jail—all of which we knew were real possibilities— then we mustn't get on the boat. (Everyone got on the boat.)
> Mary Hughes-Thompson

Dr. Bill, August 22

We are all up early before sunrise getting breakfast and doing our final packing before moving out to the boats. Derek, the first mate of the *Free Gaza*, says our departure will be at eight o'clock sharp, GMT.

"GMT?" I ask.

"Yeah, Greek maybe time."

We are back and forth, on and off the boats several times. Dr. Papadoupolous, the Cypriot head of Medecins du Monde has come through with some medical supplies from his office yesterday at the last moment. These are office pharmaceuticals that I spend time labeling as "medical cargo" and stowing below deck on the *Liberty*. Things get frantic with last minute details immediately before our departure.

Time ran out for Alice, Michael and Rashid, who had to return to the UK before the boats were ready to leave Cyprus. Time also ran out for Monir who decided he would fly to Jordan and try to get into Gaza through Erez.

Osama, who traveled with the boats from their hidden harbors around Athens, to Crete, and on to Cyprus, will now stay ashore with Ramzi and be part of the land crew.

Hedy Epstein had a medical incident just a few days before the departure of the two boats from Cyprus to Gaza. In deference to the concerns for her health expressed by boat passengers, Hedy decides not to board the ship. Hedy will later say that she will regret this decision the rest of her life.

Petros, August 21

Today is the big day. Starting at 05:00, the passengers begin gathering at the pier inside the guarded checkpoint. (We Greeks slept on the boat, our home.) There are international media people at the dock. Cypriot authorities perform the last formal checks. You can see that they welcome our mission wholeheartedly. "We are with you," one of them whispers in my ear.

Captain Giorgos and Nikos aboard *Liberty* are seriously dealing with a gas line. That means a bit more delay. We ask *Free Gaza* to move out first. There's a new captain aboard: Captain John from the US. Zacharias took the plane back home to Crete.

Dr. Bill

Good-byes are bid between those staying ashore and those going aboard several times. Finally at about 9:00 A.M. the lines are pulled in, and the *Free Gaza* and *Liberty* head out only to be stopped for two hours, because the *Liberty* needs to be repaired again.

Finally, the vessels make a half circle inside the marina with final send off from cheering supporters on the shore, and then head out past the yellow Cypriot submarine at the end of the quay and out to open sea.

For our own safety, the Cypriot Coast Guard is formally escorting our vessels into international waters. We can only

135

hope that maritime law will be respected, and that we will not be touched by the Israeli Navy in international waters.

Petros on board the *Liberty*

Nikos and Giorgos are done with the repair and they start the engine. We come out of the harbor at a low speed. The Cypriot patrol vessel escorts us out to a distance of six miles within Cypriot territorial waters. The weather is slightly worse than when we set sail from Greece. It is around four on the Beaufort scale, westerly, and it causes our boats to rock, making the new passengers rather seasick. They lie down, and we tell them what to do. No one is whining though, and that's a good start. Dr. Bill just barfed all over the stern, and looks pale and weak. So I have to mop up after him.

Dr. Bill on board the *Liberty*

First there is widespread euphoria on board, but as the sea gets deeper and rougher this joy evolves into widespread queasiness. *Free Gaza* is within eyesight of us on the *Liberty* at all times, though we are never close enough to see how its passengers are faring. We are told to eat small quantities of food frequently to curb seasickness. Many of us end up heaving our cookies anyway.

Dr. Anastasios Kourakis is a university pediatrician and a member of the Greek Parliament. He is certainly one of most important VIPs on our boats en route to Gaza. Right now, he is showing more of his human frailty as he, too, succumbs to seasickness.

We are all wearing life vests. And we have lines fastened to the boat for just this situation, which we can hook onto someone's life vest, so he or she won't inadvertently fall overboard while heaving his or her guts out. I hook Dr.

Anastasios's vest to the line. When he is done being sick, I outfit him with a Transdermal Scopolamine patch and he takes a nap. Before leaving the US, I had my family practice partner in my office write a prescription for me for ten of these patches to treat seasickness. We have five aboard the Free Gaza and five aboard here on the *Liberty*.

You would think that the eastern Mediterranean would be a boater's paradise in August. Not necessarily so, especially if you are out here in open waters, where there are no islands to buffer the waves. The Greek islands are one thing, but out here, hot air blowing up off the Sinai desert like Santa Ana winds in California can whip up the choppy seas and cause commotion with your inner being. I am starting to feel a bit queasy myself. Perhaps I can distract myself by staying busy.

I am at the stern of the boat, sorting through medical supplies with Edith Lutz from Germany, who has a nursing background and who will be my assistant if we have medical or trauma casualties on *Liberty*. Kathy Sheetz, RN, has similar responsibilities on *Free Gaza*.

My queasiness seems manageable for a while, but then it overwhelms me quite suddenly and I barf all over the back of the boat. Fortunately, our medical supplies are spared, but the deck on the stern is a mess. Petros Giotis, a Greek organizer for our Free Gaza movement has better sea legs than I. I am as weak as a kitten. He comments about how I look pale and escorts me to a mattress at mid ship to where the pitch of the seas is minimal. Petros grabs the mop and cleans up after me. Physician, treat thyself. I can't help others if I can't cope with the elements myself. I peel the plastic off the second seasick patch in our stock and put it on.

Just keep your eye on the horizon. Watch and feel the boat see-saw back and forth and to and fro like a bucking bronco and just pretend you are on some kind of amusement park ride for an extended period of time; say, 30 hours or so of stomach churning excitement. And take lots of naps. That's important.

Eventually I am able to get a handle on my seasickness, but the seas keep getting rougher and rougher. Fortunately, seasickness is the only thing I have had to treat on this boat so far. The sun sets in the west as we continue to bounce through whitecaps heading south.

Now we have southern Lebanon abeam on the portside. We can see nothing, not even city lights, because we are far out at sea, making sure we stay in international waters. For a while, other boats cross our path in and out of the ports of Beirut and other cities in southern Lebanon. Soon the border with northern Israel is abeam.

Paul Larudee is trying to contact Cyprus by satellite phone. The phones worked earlier today, but now neither one is working. We still have contact by walkie-talkie with the *Free Gaza*. They tell us that their phones are also down.

"So what does that tell you?" Paul asks. "The Israelis have all of our communications systems jammed, and now we are cut off from the world."

This is a real disappointment, since we have invested tens of thousands of dollars in sophisticated, real-time Internet streaming equipment in order to stay in touch with the world, and now none of it is working. The Israeli's seem to be acing us in the technology-tennis match.

We settle in and try to sleep through a long night of choppy seas. The sight of the lights of *Free Gaza* following us is reassuring; otherwise it could be quite lonely out here. We see the lights of other ships coming and going in and out of the Port of Haifa. We keep a close eye on them to make sure that none are trying to approach us. Nikos Bolos, the Greek first mate says the sea forecast is for things to continue getting worse before they get better.

By midnight, things are getting so rough that it becomes dangerous to move about. I nearly get tossed trying to make it back to mid ship from the stern.

"Sit down!" Yiannis Karipidis screams at me, "Or we will

put you below deck!"

No time to be polite right now. This real and present danger finally penetrates my muddled consciousness. I sit down. We are at serious risk of being thrown overboard in the darkness if we move about. "I am sorry," I shout back in order to be heard in high winds.

We all fully expect that the Israeli Navy will show up in the next few hours, latch on to our boats, haul us all in to one of their ports and arrest us. We feel resigned to this probability, but are too tired by the long day's events to feel scared. I drift in and out of short fits of sleep waiting for the sun to rise.

Mary on board the *Free Gaza*

During the dark hours of that long, cold thirty-plus-hour voyage, we expected at any moment that masked, armed frogmen would swarm the boat. At one point we were all told to gather one small piece of important baggage and assemble on deck because we had reason to think we would be boarded within twenty minutes. We stood on deck, destroying phone numbers, hiding memory cards, in anticipation of the arrival of Israeli Navy frogmen.

After the unbearable heat of Cyprus during the weeks we waited for our boats, I was unprepared for that long, wet, cold, dark night on board the *Free Gaza*. I huddled inside the Zodiac on deck, covering myself with pieces of cardboard to try to stay dry and to get a little sleep. The sea was so rough it was impossible to walk without holding onto something, and we stumbled and slid around the small space, trying not to fall as we climbed over fellow passengers, many of them seasick. For a while we were cut off from all outside communication, except from occasional shouts from our fellow boat, *Liberty*, which stayed close. Some of us looked out into the darkness for signs of Israeli gunboats, since the Israeli Foreign Office had threatened it would not let us pass. Jeff (Halper) told us we wouldn't see our attackers until they suddenly swarmed on board. It was so cold. And dark. I lay on the bottom of the Zodiac and looked up at the stars, praying I would soon see morning light.

Greta on board the *Free Gaza*

We had really sick people. One passenger almost needed to be airlifted from the deck of the boat, and we were loath to ask the Israelis for help. Thanks to the ministrations of Kathy and Sharyn, who sat up all night tending to her and forcing fluids down her throat, she ended up not totally dehydrated.

Mary sat in the Zodiac, the small boat used for emergencies that was lashed to the deck. She genteelly threw up in biodegradable rubber gloves, carefully tying each one off before handing them to me to throw overboard, several gloves bobbing in the sea, like breadcrumbs by Hansel and Gretel.

Seasickness is widespread on board the Free Gaza.

Some of the passengers already had their sea legs and managed to cheer up the rest of us by telling us it would get better. As long as I could see the horizon, I was OK. When it got dark, it was better, since we couldn't really see ourselves tossing about like a gigantic cork with a pin in it (we had a huge mast but no sail, so the mast threw us from side to side, sometimes dipping almost into the sea before righting the boat). Out of the 25 people on board, 18 were sick, sicker and sickest.

Fathi, our dear cameraman, and the cameraman from Al Jazeera were both too sick to stand up and record anything useable, but Fathi was determined he would at least hold onto the camera for dear life just in case we were boarded.

Those of us who had our sea legs were asked to take 2-hour guard duty throughout the night. At 1:00 am, David Schermerhorn and I took the duty only to find that Captain John and Derek were both too ill to pilot the boat. Ken had taken over and decided that he was going to be the new captain and demanded that I, as one of the steering committee members appoint him the new captain. I refused. David and Vik took over, and Ken stomped off downstairs into the hold, mumbling to himself. Now we had a mutiny on our hands, passengers were sick, and we were bobbing about in pitch darkness.

Ren Tawil on board the *Free Gaza*

I was used to thinking that the Mediterranean Sea was so much smaller than the Atlantic Ocean that one could appreciate the difference once setting sail on the smaller body; yet the Mediterranean is indeed an ocean in its own right both in terms of size and tempest. And within one hour, I was vomiting what little I had in my stomach as the vessel rocked and pitched without end.

With the setting sun I was retching my empty innards over

141

the side. But we all faithfully took care of each other, making sure to keep some solid food in our tummies at all times, to getting enough water, and keeping our life jackets on when not going below. The rolling motion was bad enough to force the sickest to tether themselves before leaning over the rail.

As was the case on land, the deck bristled with electronics—cell phones continually charging, laptops being used to monitor media signals, and anything that pertained to our voyage, in addition to more standard equipment for the crew to navigate and keep an ear to all other passing traffic.

Dr. Bill on board the *Liberty*

The sun finally rose and still, we see no warships on the horizon. The sea calms a bit. Now, Tel Aviv is abeam, then later, cities like Ashdod and finally Ashkelon. The passengers on the other boat report that the Ramattan news crewmembers now have a satellite phone that is working. They have found out that the Cypriot and Greek governments have launched formal protests demanding to know the status and whereabouts of the FG boats, which are registered as Greek vessels. The Arab League has launched a formal protest and is getting involved on our behalf as well. This is all good news.

We are told that a boat full of international journalists is sailing out to meet us from the Israeli port of Ashkelon. We hear that CNN will be sending a helicopter from Israel that will fly overhead to cover our efforts to reach Gaza. We wait for hours, but neither boat full of journalists nor chopper from the sky show up. Still no Israeli warships on the horizon either; only us: two synchronous sailing vessels out here on the wide blue horizon. Maybe no news is good news or maybe not. We will have to keep on moving and see.

Now we are just outside of Gaza's territorial waters at twenty nautical miles. It is 15:30, and we could be in Gaza port in just over two hours if we go for it.

Our two boats circle each other slowly while we have a pow-wow out here at sea by radio with each other. Ramattan on board the *Free Gaza* is in touch by satellite phone with members of the Popular Committee against the Siege in Gaza City. Large crowds are beginning to assemble in the port, and they want us to come in right now. Paul and Vangelis on board the *Liberty* think we should stay out at sea overnight until tomorrow morning, because if Israel apprehends us now as the sun is going down, there will be less news coverage available to us in the dark, and we will be more vulnerable if we go now as a result. The debate goes back and forth between the two boats for another half hour and tensions rise.

Finally, the *Free Gaza* crew declares, "We have got seasick passengers, and we are going in!" We see the Free *Gaza* stern getting smaller as it heads away from us toward the port. We continue to debate amongst ourselves whether we should follow them.

We finally conclude that we're sitting ducks out here by ourselves, and with trepidation, we head full speed ahead into Gaza territorial waters, hoping for the best. Fortunately, the *Liberty* is a faster vessel than the *Free Gaza*. We are able to catch up and close ranks with them over the next hour.

We are told that Gaza fishing vessels have left Gaza port to come out and escort us in. Later we hear they have been turned back by Israeli warships.

Soon we are ten nautical miles from the shoreline, well within Gaza territorial waters; still, no warships on our horizons. Where are they? Finally we get a call from *Free Gaza*....Ramattan is reporting that Israeli foreign minister Tzipi Livni has just issued an official statement declaring that Israel will not intercept the boats. The growing international pressure from around the world has lifted the siege for the first time in forty-one years! The seas grow calmer and euphoria again builds among our passengers.

Sharyn Lock, on board the *Free Gaza*

We left Cyprus August 22, in the morning, and were very lucky to have it and the following day be the only two slightly cloudy days I've experienced onboard. Because normally, there simply wasn't enough shade for twenty-four of us above deck on the *Free Gaza*, and below was steaming hot. The sea was good in sailors' terms but enough so that most people were a little sick and about eight were very sick. Working as a medic with former nurse Kathy turned out to be the perfect job for me.

I spent most of the night feeling a little queasy unless lying flat on the deck, but one of my comrades was so ill all night that we had to give her dialoryte at fifteen-minute intervals most of the night. I simply lay down beside her, drowsing in between dosing her, observing our fantastic crew (including the wondrous O.J. and Vik, who along with me, learned the basics of piloting) as they stepped over me and Donna to keep the *Free Gaza* going through the night in two-hour watches.

By early evening, we were getting what I considered the best quality Channel 16 harassment of the trip. Channel 16 is the emergency channel that must always be kept unobstructed. But ever since sailing from Greece there'd been regular strange messages in Hebrew, as well as Arabic music being played to us. This time, someone was just repeating "They're lost. They're lost." Simple yet very sinister under the circumstances!

Who was lost? Us...the *Liberty*? But we could see their lights. Or could we? Was that really the *Liberty*? And if it was, did it still have people aboard? How could we be sure, because for long stretches at a time, we couldn't contact each other. Never trust technology. I tell you we had it all—satellite phones, radios, and extremely expensive satellite Internet and video streaming—to little benefit. The video streaming had apparently been sabotaged pretty thoroughly from long distances before we even set sail, though we had some capability sometimes; everything else stopped working on both boats shortly after the "they are lost" broadcast.

We were no longer able to use the normal sea communication systems even for SOS messages. We heard later that the Greek government, wondering how the MP they sent with us was doing, had tried every method to contact us, and eventually decided we must have been sunk. Before the communications system went down however, we'd heard that media coverage had taken off and that the Arab League had announced its support of us, and stated that Israel must act in every way to protect our peaceful mission. Then there was silence.

But we had two secret weapons: our walkie-talkies, apparently too low tech to be sabotaged, that allowed us to talk between boats, and the two journalists onboard (Mr. Ramattan and Mr. Aljazeera) who had working satellite phones and had kept them off, so that Israel could not intercept their signals. Using this, we put out a press release announcing the apparent sabotage and calling particularly on the Greek government to protect us as we were sailing under Greek flags. (Actually we were sailing under about fifty flags, including a Free Leonard Peltier one, but you know what I mean.)

Morning was a blessing. Everyone cheered up, I felt fine again, and the sick people attempted some dry Greek bread. The amazingly cheerful Lauren stopped juggling walkie-talkies, and made yet another round of tea. (Let me apologize now for thinking her most useful role was going to be being related to Tony Blair.)

The working satellite phone began ringing and didn't stop: Musheir giving interviews in Arabic, Vik in Italian, and Jeff in Hebrew. We began to put up more flags. Messages came in about whether a media boat was coming or not coming from Israel to meet up with us. We kept grabbing passing crew and asking them how many hours until we left ?

Then, having established contact again with the *Liberty*, we had an argument with them, miles out from Gaza territorial waters. Paul and Vangelis wanted to stop, postpone entering Gaza waters— our most dangerous stretch to cross in terms of potential Israeli attack—until the next morning, so we'd avoid the greater risk of attack at night.

But we on *Free Gaza* weren't interested. If we weren't stopped, we'd reach Gaza in three hours, and there would still be three hours until dusk. We called our Gaza hosts. "Yalla!" [Come now], they said. Technically we had a steering committee of three on our boat; Greta, Musheir and Jeff; and two on the *Liberty*. But the "discussion" was happening on walkie-talkie, which made it impossible. We'd created an odd numbered steering committee to vote if they had to, and as I saw it (clinging to some semblance of process), that's what we'd just defaulted to: our entire boat including three steering committee members, wanted to go ahead. The *Liberty* asked for an hour to talk.

"No," said the *Free Gaza*, that hour's daylight can't be wasted—we're off.

And we did the boat equivalent of stomping off. I don't dare imagine what the *Liberty* thought of us at that point, as we watched them get smaller and smaller.

Aki Nawaz on board the *Liberty*

We sailed with many thoughts, but the talk was about being shot at by the IDF and which bag should the body parts go into. Nature's way took its toll as the heat drained us, but we were close and Gaza was two days away. The sea was also testing many with its waves dismantling the inner lining of our stomachs. The sight of heroes thrown around and vomiting helplessly brought home the fear factor.

The night was dark as we travelled nearer to our destination; my thoughts lost all control, body weakened by the annoying vegan food, my claustrophobia kicked in. I had forgotten about the fear.

I began to dream fitfully. My body was looking for escape. The sea must have a path for those that wish to escape. I began to hear loud hailers and warnings —the imagination felt the boot and the fist of the IOF. I was being dragged by the hair with a gun in my face —the darkness was like a dream and the body was the nightmare where it loses all energy and just cries out for death as a worthwhile escape. I felt the handcuffs tight and the darkness of a cell, no-one knew where I was, I could not breathe —I prayed to my thoughts, my body limp and boneless. Death was to be a lonely affair, no one to hold my hand or read the rites.

I had been here before in Pakistan, but this time, it was certain. Life flashed by, as I opened my eyes and saw Bill the doctor, attempting some words to help. I realized he was also seeking comfort; many lay there battered by nature and not the IOF. A sudden jerk of my body, and it all came out polluting or feeding the sea with human vomit in its tri-colors, the drama of vomiting always exaggerating my body movements into almost an epileptic dance. Tired and worn out, I put my head down and just gave up to sleep and whatever would come of us.

The sound of arguments and shouting over the radio transmitter woke me up, as the sea was now rocking us in a motherly way. I had not died the night before, and it was afternoon. The passengers on the two ships who had been brothers in spirit began to disagree over the next move. We were not far from Gaza, but news had been filtering to the boats that the IOF was on our tail and that tactics would have to change. Everyone held to their own opinions and this time, the lack of a "leader," a "wise voice," led to confusion. We were close to Gaza, but the next decision could save the IOF a lot of trouble (we were, after all, our own worst enemies at this point). Some contemplated staying away till the day after and some insisted on going right now. The contemplators lost the argument, as they desperately followed the mother ship that had now pulled away and was fading into the distance.

We had seen military activity in the distance, and I quickly emptied the film tapes of the whole journey into the life jackets —surely they would not search and confiscate all the life jackets.

The atmosphere intensified between the two ships, and the calming sea was burdened by the anger on board.

Nothing could be worse than this, almost four weeks of endurance and tests, everything imaginable that could go wrong did go wrong; yet we had gotten this far, and now it looked bleak and miserable.

The people of Gaza had been awaiting our arrival for weeks; many false alarms had seen them walk away in silence from the seafront; the whole city had anticipated our arrival under impossible circumstances. For them, it was history in the making on the international platform; and we were so close, yet so far.

Dismay set in, and I really just thought everything negative about all these people who I had come to love. It became like the whole music industry; egos, back stabbing and as insincere as it could be. Yes, I was alive, but for what? The night before, I had contemplated giving it all up; and now it had given itself up.

Then, the *Liberty* began to follow the *Free Gaza* into shore.

Chapter 8: We Are Coming, We Have Arrived

Gamaal Al-Attar, Ren Tawil, Bill Dienst, Musheir El Farra, Mary Hughes Thompson, Mona El Farra, MD, Jamal El-Khoudary, Renee Bowyer, Aki Nawaz, Vittorio Arrigoni

Gamaal Al-Attar, Gaza

The sun was shining on August 23, 2008, and everyone in Gaza was waking up in order to get ready for the D Day. It is the day everyone in Gaza has been waiting for a long time; a day we will feel like there are some people in the world who care for our suffering. A day we will feel that we belong to the human race, and that our brothers and sisters in humanity care for our daily struggles. Scouts from different scout groups had signed up to be in the welcoming committee on the fishing boats. So, we headed directly to the main port of Gaza at 08:00, and together with policemen who are there to secure the crowds, we boarded the boats and started the trip to the open sea.

Hours of waiting in the boats made everyone seasick, and by noon, most of our hope flew away with the wind. It looked like the two boats were not coming. We were screwed. All the dreams and feelings that there was someone who cared for us got smaller and smaller as time went on. Jamal El Khoudari (the coordinator for the campaign) spoke at a press conference that the boats had gotten lost and made some excuse. I and the other scouts in Gaza did not want to listen to excuses. The people of Gaza wanted them here now. The smiles that were on every single face by the morning, the joyful people in the port waiting at sunrise, and the hope of seeing someone who would care for us changed into a huge disappointment. By noon, nearly everyone had left the port and gone back home.

On the way back home, I saw Gaza looking darker than ever, and a small tear escaped from my eye. "It looks like there is no one who cares for us," a boy scout told me. I opened my mouth to tell him that this wasn't true, but I could not find a word to say.

Just like all the scouts, I went home, took a shower, and tried to rest after a long day under heavy sun. All of us were seasick and sick in our hearts as well. I lay on my bed to sleep and forget about humankind. I set my head on my pillow and thought. "We are on our own, and nobody cares."

Then my mum came to my room with a smile on her face, "Jamal, the boats are visible on TV." So I jumped from my bed and asked her, "When?" She said, "It is just breaking news." I can't remember how, when, or why I found myself on a bus going back to the port with the scouts. I can't remember how we managed to be together again going to the Port of Gaza. We all jumped on board different fishing boats and sailed to the open sea again. There, on the horizon, I saw three elements: A beautiful sunset, the SS *Liberty*, and the SS *Free Gaza*. On the east side of the Port, more and more people from Gaza were gathering. This time, their disappointed faces were not there. We could hear the people laughing high and delighted as they strained to catch sight of the boats.

In a couple of minutes, those of us on the fishing boats came closer to the *Free Gaza*, and I saw the peace flag hanging up, and Maria Del Mar Fernandez waving a Palestinian flag and shouting. Suddenly, I saw many kids taking off their t-shirts and jumping into the sea, swimming to the *Free Gaza*. My small boat got me closer to the boats, and as my feet touched the deck, it gave me a shock. My mind was blown away as I forgot every single suffering I had in my life under Israel's blockade. I moved over to someone who was so calm and a bit away from all the media.

"Hey, welcome to Gaza." I said with a smile.

I kept repeating these words and getting happier with every handshake. By the side of the cabin, I saw a muscled guy with Tattoos on his arms and a nice cap. "Is he the captain?" I wondered. After shaking his hand, I kept speaking to him, and within moments, we became friends. He was this nice Italian guy who had left Italy searching for justice and truth whose name was Vittorio Utopia Arrigoni. I shared the Palestinian flag with him, and we started waving to the media and the tens of thousands of people who came to see the boats in our small port.

For a short period, the boats orbited inside the marina; then it was time to evacuate the boats and to greet our guests on land in Gaza. We scouts stood in a line and saluted the new Palestinians who had come from across the globe with one message, "Stay Human".

I will never forget all the small and big hands that came out from the crowds to shake hands with the activists. I can't forget how tanned the people were after that very long waiting day in the port, but also I can't forget the spirit in the crowd after those heroes landed on the shore. I remember I went home that day with a charged battery for life and hope. The two boats weren't necessarily bringing supplies to the people of Gaza, but they brought what is more important. They brought enough hope for over 1.5 million people who live under the blockade that someday we would be free.

Ren, on board the *Free Gaza*

The high point came with word that the Israeli Ministry of Information, after repeated warnings that Israeli forces will never permit our landing in Palestine, announced that now they will leave us alone, ostensibly due to the nature of our action being "humanitarian" and "peaceful". The real reason for this 180-degree decision had much more to do with anticipated world criticism of Israel if they tried to stop us

Earlier, a formal letter addressed to Free Gaza movement from their information minister concluded that, because our shipment of aid and our intent to carry back Arab passengers was being carried out directly between FG and Gaza's "outlawed" Hamas government, our actions must be deemed as support of terrorism. Their reversal of position on this was clearly a public relations-oriented contradiction of a very long standing policy.

Two to three hours later, the coastline at last appeared after we spotted an imposing smokestack to the north—Ashkelon, Israel. Just as we began to make out the harbor's opening at Gaza City, a speedboat with four men raced toward us, frantically waving, and all smiles; another soon followed, then the welcoming committees' watercraft grew bigger and bigger, each one bristling with the natives, circling our vessels, weaving in and out.

The emotional climax came with the sighting of the breakwater's endless masses of cheering Gazans, 40,000 strong. Children dove from the boats into the polluted water far from shore, eagerly grabbing for the balloons that we had started blowing up an hour earlier and tossed into the bay. Then, as if to seal the two-year promise by FG to close the gap and make Palestine's sea route open once and for all, the boats sidled up to *Free Gaza* and *Liberty* and spilled their teary-eyed passengers onto our deck, who then embraced us as if we were liberating soldiers.

Dr. Bill on board the *Liberty*

"Land ahoy!" Someone shouts. We scan the shore with our binoculars. We are now inside three nautical miles, and then the Gaza City skyline gradually enlarges in front of us. In spite of all the hardships during the past few years, Gaza shines like an emerald at this moment from the bow as we head in.

As we get closer, the reality becomes clearer. Gaza is overcrowded. To the north, we see the coal-fired power plant across the border in Ashkelon, Israel, then the crowded cinderblock buildings of Beach Refugee Camp, then more sturdy high-rise buildings and towering minarets in the Rimal district of Gaza City, and then wall-to-wall inhabitation all the way south as far as we can see beyond the town and refugee camp of Deir Al Balah. Now we can pick out the marina. And there are fishing boats packed with Gazans coming out to greet us! The breakwater is packed wall-to wall with people cheering. (Later estimates put the crowd at about 40 thousand.)

It is if we were astronauts returning from the moon. After all, each and every one of the Apollo astronauts has been to the moon and back, and an additional three and a half decades have passed since the last humans have arrived from international waters into Gaza Port.

Entering the port to sheer joy, jubilation and pandemonium!

Hundreds of boys are swimming out to our boats from the shore, as local fishing boats encircle us. It looks chaotic and dangerous, especially for the fearless young boys in the water. I am hoping no one gets hit and injured by a vessel or its propeller. Several dignitaries come aboard our vessels via the fishing boats, and we are served tea and coffee while we attach a ladder to the sides of our boats to accept those who have swum out to us from shore. A Boy Scout band plays for us from an adjacent boat. Pretty soon, both boats are jam-packed with people all over the deck and on the roof above. There has to be a limit. We haven't even docked yet, and it is difficult to see how we will get through all the crowds in the water to do so.

Finally, the police detail starts coming aboard our vessels to do crowd control and limit further boarding of our boats. Our vessels ease their way through the local fishing boats and people in the water and finally reach their moorings. We slowly disembark and are escorted through the dense crowds and onto buses that will take us a couple blocks up the beach to the El Deira Hotel, our new home while we are in Gaza. We are pressing the flesh like crazy and hugging all the children all the way to the bus. A woman gives me a sash made of green fabric with Arabic writing and places it over my head like I am some sort of war hero. I say, "Shukran" [thank you]. We all gain insight about what it must be like to be famous politicians, rock musicians, or members of a sports team.

Musheir El Farra, on board the *Free Gaza*

As Gaza started to appear on the horizon, I felt ecstatic; I just could not believe it. I never expected it. After all the threats, I thought we would end up in an Israeli prison. I could not stop my tears. At last, I will be able to visit my mother, Laila's grave. Laila always said to people around her, even when she was in good health, "If I die, please tell Musheir that the last words on

154

my lips were his name." Yet I couldn't be at her bedside when she was dying at the hospital where I was born, because of this inhuman and illegitimate siege. My tears continued. Greta was standing next to me. She hugged me, and, in a very emotional voice said, "Musheir, these moments can never be taken away from us."

As we neared the coast, Derek, one of our colleagues, came to me asking to contact the Gaza Port authorities to seek permission to enter Gaza's territorial waters. No international ships had docked in Gaza Port since 1967, so the port authorities did not know how to guide us. By then I could see Gaza clearly. I erupted: "No need, there is the Beach Camp, there is Omar Al Mukhtar Street. I can see Al Shohada Street. The port is there, right in front of us."

We continued towards the port until our dream came true. We had reached Gaza against all the odds.

Seated: Greta (in sunglasses), Ren, Kathleen, Courtney, Musheir, waving on the right and Fathi with camera, overjoyed Palestinians holding balloons and cheering behind us.

155

Without a doubt our arrival was a breath of freedom and hope for the people of the Gaza Strip. The thousands waiting for us, every one in the Gaza Strip felt a sense of pride during those euphoric moments. It was a feeling of dignity that comes from defiance when much of the world, including Arab regimes, turns a blind eye to the Palestinians' suffering. Even if we had only achieved a few moments of triumph for the people, this would have been a good enough cause.

On the morning that the Break the Siege boats were due to depart from Gaza port, I woke up very early. I went to Khan Younis cemetery with my colleague, Fathi Jouadi, to visit my mother's grave. It was the first time I had visited the grave. I spontaneously found myself talking to my mother. I could not stop my tears, saying,

"Mother, I am here. I am visiting you despite their siege." I used to joke with my mother. "Do not die when I cannot be with you." She would laugh and say, "Don't worry, I will not if you promise to place me in my grave with your own hands." I had promised to do that, but was unable to.

It was a great feeling, a feeling of freedom that I had never experienced. It was the first time in my life that I had visited home without the humiliation of being questioned or interrogated by the Israelis, without being threatened, having my travel documents thrown in my face, and not knowing whether I would be able to get out or not. It is a sense of liberation I hope every Palestinian will experience one day. I am proud of being one of the first Palestinians from the Occupied Territories to enter Palestine without Israeli permission since 1967. [1]

Mary on board the *Free Gaza*

Finally, slowly our little boats kept on chugging toward Gaza. At one point we were told we expected to be boarded within twenty minutes, so we each packed our smallest backpack with

156

our most important possessions. We destroyed anything we had that might be dangerous for us or for our friends in Palestine if it fell into Israeli hands. The 20 minutes came and went, and another hour, and another. Greta whispered to me "I think they might not stop us..." and I breathed "Insha'Allah."[6]

Somebody shouted: "Gaza!" and we all rushed to the railing and saw the misty shore of Gaza far off on the horizon. We were euphoric. We were almost there. And we hadn't seen an Israeli gunboat. Another hour and the shores of Gaza became clearer; we could see buildings. Suddenly I heard shouting and I saw a small boat approaching, a couple of young men waving Palestinian flags, smiling and screaming. We started to inflate the red, white, green and black balloons we had brought along, each showing a dove and the words "Free Palestine." We threw them in the water and saw there were three boats, and six, and a dozen, and one that even had a brass band playing to welcome us. Boys were in the water all around us, diving for balloons, and then clambering onto our decks. I feared they might drown, or that our little boat might sink.

We couldn't believe it was real. Larger boats came to greet us. Then we were in Gaza Port. Thousands of people stood along the wharf to greet us... men, women, children... all waving, all shouting, smiling. Palestinian flags everywhere. A band played a welcome. Our friend Dr. Mona El Farra came on board to be greeted by her brother Musheir who had sailed on the *Free Gaza*. It seemed as though all of Gaza was there. We hugged each other and were hugged by strangers.

We were led through the crowds and onto land. As Vittorio knelt and embraced the ground of Gaza, we shared his joy! We were in Gaza at last. That was the moment when we all became Palestinian.

---

[6] "If God wills it." A common exclamation in Arabic

Next morning I awoke in my hotel room and tried to register what had happened. I was so afraid I was dreaming, as I had often dreamed of waking up one day in Gaza. I touched the walls, I looked at Greta sleeping, I peered through the window and saw the beach, fishermen setting off in the early light, and then I spied our two little boats bobbing up and down. And I dared to believe it was true.

I sent an email to my friends who were waiting for news:

I woke up this morning wondering if it was all a dream. And then I looked through the window and saw the harbor, and the fishing boats, and our two proud little boats, *Free Gaza* and *Liberty*, bobbing gently in the Gaza breeze and I could finally believe we are here!

There are not enough words to describe the feelings we all had as we saw the shores of Gaza appear on our horizon, and then as we got closer and closer we were welcomed by the first of dozens of fishing boats, all crowded with cheering, waving Gazans who had waited since early morning for our arrival.

Dozens of them jumped into the water and climbed aboard our boats, cheering and waving and hugging everybody, smiling and telling us "you are welcome." I don't know how so many members of our welcoming committee managed to crowd onto the wharf.... women, men, children, a band playing for us and police trying to control them as more of them jumped into the water to reach us.

It was truly an experience for a lifetime. Surreal! After two years of planning and hoping, and disappointments, and great sadness when our beloved friend Riad was suddenly gone from us. But his spirit is here with us, and many of us wore pink shirts in his memory.

There is so much more to say, but for now this is just to say we have arrived, we are elated, and we are humbled; we could not have achieved this without the support of so many friends and strangers who believed in us. Shukran, and love to all of you.

Mary in Gaza City

One of the things that most amazed me was that so many people were there to greet us, even though the ones I asked told me they felt sure the Israelis would stop our boats. When news reached them that we had set sail from Cyprus they started to gather in Gaza City, forty thousand of them, determined to be there just in case a miracle happened.

They waited there for hours. And the miracle happened.

Dr. Mona El Farra, waiting in Gaza

It was a hot summer day in Gaza. I was at the humble port of Gaza at 7 A.M. on August 23, with the team of the Palestinian International Campaign to End the Siege. I was so excited, anxious and exhausted. But I would never give up hope that those brave 44 pioneering men and women, who were trying to break the siege, would make it.

We had lost communications with them and had heard that all radio transmissions were cut off. I had conflicting feelings; worried, afraid for their safety. My brother was on one of those boats! As time passed, the huge crowds who were waiting gave up and left the beach. I stayed with a few people, not willing to give up hope that we would soon see them over the horizon. I was feeling hot, sweaty and tired, trying to cheer up the people next to me, talking about the impact of publicity of this great act of solidarity by people from around the world. Even if they did not make it to Gaza, it was a big victory for solidarity and for the activists who tried to reach us.

My heart was roaring with conflicting feelings, "Oh my God! Will they stay alive? What is next? What will the Israeli reaction be like?" We waited and we waited as the afternoon sun bore down on us.

All of a sudden in the far horizon of the lovely sea of Gaza, I could see two tiny strange and moving objects. Somebody shouted, "It's the boats! It's the Free Gaza movement boats!"

In disbelief, I ran to the far end of the port shouting and chanting, "Free free Palestine." I was dancing with joy, watching the boats coming closer and closer. Crowds started to pour into the port, spontaneous, happy and excited. I hurried to try to go onboard one of the small Gaza fishing boats.

It was difficult; all of a sudden, I was picked up and carried by some fishermen. I found myself on a small boat while the Free Gaza boats entered the harbor. I was waving, stretching my hands, crying and laughing at the same time. Then I was carried by the same fishermen and found myself on board the *Free Gaza*, hugging Greta, Mary and my brother, Musheir. For me it was a historic moment; I was proud, relieved and full of joy.

We are not alone; we are not forgotten. I thought, "They made it, and one day, Palestinian people will make it and be free. It will happen."

This experience makes me think deeper about the importance of people's solidarity with Palestine, and how we should always strengthen this bond, and fight together against all sorts of injustices small or large. It is a day I will never forget.

MP Jamal El-Khoudary waiting in Gaza

The day they arrived sailing from Cyprus to the port of fishermen in the Gaza Strip was joyful, as we welcomed them.

I was always sure that their trip would succeed, because it had all the elements of success: the noble will, the ongoing work, sacrifice, teamwork, persistence and determination. These reasons made the ships *Liberty* and *Free Gaza* break the siege for the first time since 1967. That moment was a defining one in the course of the siege. All Gazans: men, women and children, even our elderly people celebrated the arrival of these 44 activists. They wanted to shake hands with them, to sit with them, to talk to them. Their arrival had laid the foundation to break the siege.

Words can never express our gratitude and appreciation to each one of the activists. They came from different countries and different religions, they were young and they were old, they had braved the sea and the threats; and they agreed on one goal, defending the oppressed and the weak, the people with no voice. And they stood up with us in the face of the occupier.

We thank all the activists whom we shall never forget. On that day, they made history!

Renee Bowyer on board the *Liberty*

There was a moment on the 23rd August 2008, sometime after 3 pm, when I suddenly realized I was going to reach Gaza.

Up until that moment the idea had been a dream-never far from my consciousness but still very much a dream. For two years I and my crazy sea-faring friends had done all sorts of things to try and make this journey happen; had held secret meetings in the bombed out streets of Dahiya, in Southern Lebanon, and put letters under stage doors of famous people acting in London's West End in the hope that they might want to come along; we had spent the years trying to convince people that we really would save enough pennies to buy a boat and sail to Gaza.

But I had said it so many times in so many strange and coded ways. (I remember after talking to Riad on the phone. Sometimes I used to wonder if I was not really involved in some project for assessing the likelihood of acquiring double-decker buses to be used in areas of Beirut, rather than buying a boat.) It had become almost like something that was going to happen but only in the future.

The frustrating, agonizing and brilliantly entertaining three weeks we spent in Cyprus, inventing ways to keep ourselves occupied (like hand-sewing banners), and our thoughts away from the possibility that the boats weren't actually coming, suggested to me that the moment might never be realized- the moment of knowing we would see Gaza from atop a rolling wave.

But then that moment came. We got the 'all clear' from the radio and everyone on board the boat started repeating to everyone else that the Israeli's were not going to come; they were not going to stop us.

The only thing that was between us and Gaza was the clear rolling sea. I remember staring toward the shore waiting for the first sight of the land while Gaza was still hidden by the horizon haze. But even in the midst of that joy, images of Gaza were haunting me. What would we find when we reached there? How scarred would the war-weary people be? Would they really care to see two fishing boats filled with very seasick passengers coming into port? People who had so many horror stories to tell...

. . . Of the little girl kneeling in anguish amongst the shattered bodies of her family, shelled while picnicking on the Gaza beach.

...Of an alleyway in Beit Hanoun running a stream of blood from the massacres of 2006.

...Of the crumpled body of a woman lying beneath the lamppost, killed while protesting the besieging of the Beit Hanoun mosque where the men were trapped inside.

...Of a little boy begging his father to shield him, and the father sitting helpless, as his protecting arms failed to stop the bullet that murdered him.

...And of a young American woman shouting at the driver of a bulldozer to stop, but he didn't, crushing her with his blade which he dropped back over her crumpled body to crush her again.

Somewhere there behind the haze was Gaza. A place filled with as many stories of tragedy and suffering as any place in the world was.

And then the horizon haze lifted and we were staring at the skyline of Gaza city itself. An involuntary cry went up from everyone on board the boat, and I can't remember whether it was with tears or laughter - both probably. Some of us were jumping up and down; some embracing, some sitting quietly. I am not sure that anyone was prepared for this or for what happened next.

We had prepared ourselves for capture, to be shelled, for our boats to sink; we had prepared ourselves for lengthy stints in Israeli prisons and the possibilities of injury. But I am not sure that we had dared prepare ourselves for the sort of greeting we were to have when we reached the people of Gaza. We hadn't really thought much about what we would do if we actually reached the shores.

I remember some time that morning, while on the boat and when there was still a whole sea between us and Gaza, that someone on board had said there were thousands of people at Gaza port waiting for our arrival - but hours and hours had passed since then. By now it was almost sunset and it had never been clear to the people of Gaza that we were going to make it; surely they had gone home . . . but when we got close enough to the shore we saw there were not just thousands of people still there, but tens of thousands. Old fishing boats spilling over with people were sailing towards us with so many happy faces onboard; there were drums beating and kids in the water, unafraid of the boats that were tossing to and fro on the swell around them.

As our boats were escorted into the port, and we were fully aware of the extent of the welcome, I don't think there was a dry eye on board either of our boats. Who were we to deserve this? What had we done or endured on the scale of what the people around us had done and endured to be given this honour?

In an era where this sort of turnout in the West only happens for film stars or sporting heroes (and in Australia, sometimes for the Queen), it came as a shock to see how different it was here. This greeting and celebration was not for an individual or for individuals, not for sporting prowess or Hollywood good looks; it was for what we represented by making that journey. I am not sure that I know exactly what we did represent to the people who came to greet us; but it had to do with civil resistance, with challenging injustice and with upholding the human right to break barriers when they were set there to imprison.

Is there any other port in the world where this could possibly happen? Where before any formalities or passport checks, customs or officials, we could be embraced as lost relatives might be by whoever was near enough to embrace us? Where we could fish sparkling eyed laughing children out of the water before we had even thrown a rope ashore? I doubt it; it was exhilarating!

On the 23rd August 2008 we were witness to a massive celebration of civil resistance. The Palestinian people showed the world that day that they were still capable of the most wholesome and forgiving of human gestures: joy; which is in itself, the supreme act of resistance. Yes, we were not just witnesses but also a part of those celebrations because, in some small way, our long journey there had allowed them to happen.

For that I will be forever humbled and grateful.

Aki Nawaz on board the *Liberty*

Moments earlier, I had been in despair. Suddenly out of the sky, a transmission arrived that the Israelis had backed down, from what I never knew. We never sought their approval, and the news was literally the biggest wave that hit us. From despair over that terrible night came joy. The whole mutiny episode was sent down into the depths of the sea, as we all jumped and hugged each other. Love had returned in all its glory, everyone was fabulous to me again; the camera switched itself on and captured the moments.

The ships swung around and held hands once more, and we prepared them as if we were the happy wedding party. The flags pointed towards Gaza. I was overwhelmed, but I wanted to see that city before it saw me. As I scrambled up to the highest point on the ship, there in the distance was utopia. This was a voyage bigger than any film; it was real. The skyline appeared and there it was, and we had broken the siege, at least for the moment. This continuous and deliberate barbaric act against humanity had been, for once, blasphemed against with righteousness and good will.

I phoned friends around the world and showed off. We had done it; they had all thought we were crazy, and they were right. Gaza began to shine and glitter as it became bigger and closer. Local fishermen and their boats had never seen happier times, as they created a carnival of sound and colors escorting us into the harbor.

Thousands stood at the seafront with the biggest and most beautiful smiles; the feeling cannot be captured by words or expression. I always hated flags as a sign of patriotic symbolism. But for once, I picked up the Pakistani flag, and waved it to the people of Gaza, to let them know that people in Pakistan carry their struggle with them everyday.

Every person on those ships as well as those that worked on this mission-impossible represent the best of humanity from all over the world. This mission really happened, and it was better than any song I could possibly write.

Sharyn after disembarking from the *Free Gaza*[2]

How can I possibly begin to coherently tell you anything of the last twenty-four hours? I can't even comprehend any of it right now, let alone communicate it. You'll just have to get it in scraps of thoughts. Yvonne and I are sitting here right now trying to think of the date yesterday. "We've made history and neither of us even knows what day we did it on," says Yvonne. "Just as well that it wasn't us running the Battle of Hastings. We'd be saying ten sixty-three or was it ten sixty-five?" We've now agreed it was August 23 yesterday, and I am very much hoping this finally gets me into the Housman's Peace Diary (without dying) even if just for next year.

Here, in a restaurant overlooking crumbling shacks on the beach, we exchanged greetings with our hosts in such a daze that I still don't know most of their names. But the important thing was we had all of them. Every group with which we'd worked was united in their support of our accomplishment. The Popular Committee against the Siege and the International Campaign to End the Siege on Gaza, the Gaza Medical Relief Society folks, the Gaza Community Mental Health Programme, and other nonpartisan groups, Hamas and Fatah reps and PFLP were present.

Huwaida even got a congratulatory call from Mahmoud Abbas, the head of government in the West Bank (not particularly legitimate, but the only one the United States talks to). For at least an hour or two, we had achieved Palestinian national unity.

The next day, just as I thought the dreamlike quality of things might at least start to disperse, some of my comrades came back from an unofficial lunch with Ismail Haniyeh, the Hamas prime minister. Many of us chose not to attend to remain clearly politically separate from any faction. My comrades announced that we would be given Palestinian citizenship.

166

And for the first time I began to cry.

Dr. Bill, August 23

All forty-four of us are taken to the El Deira Hotel and assigned rooms. Our baggage arrived later, taken off the two boats by the police after we had negotiated the chaos of dense and giant crowds in the marina. After settling in, we are hosted for a dinner reception out on the hotel veranda overlooking the beach. We can see our boats docked to the south, bobbing softly in the water about a half a kilometer away.

Vittorio Arrigoni, August 23

History is us
History is not cowardly governments
with their loyalty to whoever has the strongest military

History is made by ordinary people
everyday people, with family at home and a regular job
who are committed to peace as a great ideal
to the rights of all to staying human.

History is us who risked our lives
to bring utopia within reach
to offer a dream, a hope, to hundreds of thousands of people
Who cried with us as we reached the port of Gaza

Our message of peace is a call to action
for other ordinary people like ourselves
not to hand over your lives
to whatever puppeteer is in charge this time round

But to take responsibility for the revolution
First, the inner revolution

to give love, to give empathy
It is this that will change the world

We have shown that peace is not an impossible utopia
Or perhaps we have shown that sometimes
utopia can be possible

Believe this
Stand firm against intimidation, fear, and despair
And simply remain human.[3]

Vittorio, Captain John and Ren are overjoyed to arrive in Gaza.

Chapter 9: Getting to Know Gaza

Greta Berlin, Bill Dienst, Sharyn Lock, Lauren Booth

Greta

In all of the training we had done, the scenarios we envisioned and the counter measures we had considered, none of us had ever thought we would actually get to Gaza. Even people like me, the incurable optimists, were more concerned with prison solidarity than solidarity with the Palestinians of Gaza if we actually arrived. We had no clue what we were going to do once we arrived in Gaza. Fortunately, wiser heads in Gaza prevailed, and they designed a four-day itinerary for us. We were too stunned, sick and overwhelmed to think that far in advance. Many of us could barely walk, and stumbled from boat to hotel with our sea legs complaining that they were now on land.

Within hours of our arrival, the committees who we had worked through email for the past two years had everything arranged, down to the transportation for the next four days and the places we should visit. They had certainly thought the itinerary out better than any of us had. We were just happy to be on solid land.

169

Dr. Bill, August 24th

Our first visit this morning is to Al Shifa Hospital, the largest medical center in the Gaza Strip. It takes up several city blocks; a luxury of space as far as Gaza is concerned. Shifa is a large teaching hospital and has had the full spectrum of primary care and specialty services, which are starting to fall apart. But like other hospitals in Gaza, the problem is not lack of knowledge. Gaza physicians have been trained all over the world. Since the siege, further training abroad is drying up because it is becoming more difficult for medical students and residents from Gaza to come and go. In Gaza, the current problem is deterioration of the medical infrastructure due largely to the tightening siege.

We are taken to the medical oncology unit, where they have fully trained oncologists, but now a markedly limited stock of cancer chemotherapy drugs, which are rationed by Israel from outside. For example, when there are several patients with similar cancer diagnoses who need a particular course of chemotherapy, the doctors must choose between giving one patient a full course of treatment and denying it to others or giving all patients incomplete courses of treatment limited by the on-again-off-again interruption in supplies coming in through Israel.

Over in the dialysis unit there are similar stories of deteriorating infrastructure. Patients who previously received dialysis three times per week are now limited to once per week. They are getting weaker because they have to wait longer for limited dialysis machines to purge the normal metabolic poisons from their bodies. This leads to further medical complications that could be mitigated through more frequent dialysis. Meanwhile, there are dialysis machines sitting up against the wall that are dormant because of a lack of reagents and repair parts to maintain them. In the surgical unit the breakdown of the system is similar. There are not enough

170

anesthetic and surgical supplies to keep up with demand. Even though there are surgeons capable of doing the operations, the operations are not getting done because of the lack of essential supplies.

The breakdown of medical services due to the siege increased the need for Gazans with certain medical problems to travel abroad; efforts being blocked by the Israelis. According to the Gaza Ministry of Health, as of August, 2008, over 250 Palestinians have died while waiting through endless Israeli bureaucratic delays denying them exit to Egypt, Israel, Jordan, or other places for subspecialty care currently not available in Gaza. There are thousands of medical patients with time-sensitive illnesses whose lives are being directly threatened by the siege. There are also thousands of Gaza students whose hopes and future livelihoods are being destroyed by the siege.

After visiting Shifa, most of us take a bus north to a large assembly hall in the middle of Shati (Beach) refugee camp. The hall is surrounded by cinderblock apartments, with windows filled by the faces of local residents. They look down from their windows on us in the assembly hall, and the proceedings begin. There is an abundance of still and movie cameras capturing our event with the prime minister.

This is a social event, not a political event, and we at Free Gaza are determined that it remain social, much like a dinner with the President of the U.S. would be, and we are delighted to have lunch with Haniyeh.

Ismail Haniyeh speaks to us through his English interpreter. He describes our arrival as "heroic". He bestows medals and embraces each of us. Up close he appears to be a very charismatic teddy bear. Even those in Gaza who dislike Hamas speak fondly of this prime minister. He does not live in a mansion, like the other prime minister in the West Bank. He lives among the people right here in Beach camp. After our meeting, he takes us on a walking tour of the neighborhood so

171

we can all gain a deeper appreciation of the reality of life here in Gaza.

We visit family after family in overcrowded apartments, where people are packed to more than ten to a room. There is extremely limited room in Beach Camp for gardens or other vegetation.

Sharyn, August 25

Gaza waters extend twelve miles off the coast; after 12 miles, one is in international waters at that point. However, Israeli gunboats regularly patrol the waters at the six-mile point, shooting at any boats that cross this line; they say they are imposing this limit. (Our Greek friends find this particularly upsetting because throughout thousands of years, the Mediterranean was always free for its entire people to sail until now. This restriction makes for poor fishing: something to do with the sea being too warm for many fish that close to shore, and also it's a small area for everyone to fish in. But more to the point, Israeli gunboats don't just shoot at boats that cross this arbitrary six-mile line, but also at boats three miles out, two miles out, and even at people on the beach.)

So the *Free Gaza* and a bunch of us headed out on about five or six small wooden fishing boats. Our boats were flying a lot of our flags for the occasion, including both the American and the Australian ones flying upside down by accident rather than design, I think! We decided to go catch some fish beyond the six-mile point, steaming on to eight miles. However, not so far from the coast, the smudge skulking on the horizon suddenly began moving along what appeared to be an intercept line. It was a spiky grey Israeli ship, all angles and whirling technical things, plus deck-mounted guns.

The fishermen had been showing people multiple bullet holes in both the boats and themselves from earlier incidents. On the first little boat the speedy Israeli ship would reach,

172

Renee and I watched with adrenalin pumping a bit and climbed up to the stern in the usual tradition of being visible (which could be interpreted either as internationals in the area or here, we'll make it easier for you to shoot us).

Then another Israeli ship appeared from the other direction. A third joined them, and began to circle our little group of boats. But that turned out to be pretty much it for most of the rest of the day; six Palestinian boats fishing, three Israeli boats circling menacingly—except you can't pull off menacing for hours and hours without following it up. After it became apparent they were not going to attack, they just simply weren't that interesting anymore.

Certainly, they were not as interesting as fishing! Man, fishing is bizarre. And damn hard work. The sun blazed the whole day and the only shade was inside the wheelhouse or a few feet beside it. About five men, plus two young boys, were on the boat working, hauling nets, and winding heavy ropes and cables. It was only a small boat, with blistered paint and rusted metal, but its owner was very proud of its engine, which roared deafeningly and which he told us would go faster than the *Free Gaza* easily. It ran on bottle after bottle of cooking oil; one more thing like powered milk and in fact almost everything edible here comes through despite the Israeli siege.

How? Via the hundreds of tunnels between Gaza and Egypt. (Another reason why Israel's alleged reason for keeping the draconian siege on Gaza for 'security' reasons is a lie. Anything can come through those tunnels, including cars and cattle. Israel's siege is all about stealing Gaza's resource of the sea... its gas.)

When it came time to bring up the nets, Renee and I perched on the roaring, steaming engine's roof, combining a patch of shade with avoiding twisting ropes while going slowly deaf, and watched everyone work to raise the nets and empty them onto the boat's floor. What a spectacle of mass death! Thousands of fish of all descriptions, all flapping about

173

desperately, incredibly strange colored and shaped, all gasping their last. Disoriented crabs and small bemused octopi clambered over one another in slow drunken bewilderment, at which I wanted to laugh, but couldn't, since most were living their last moments.

The two boys slipped about among the fish, examining the odder ones and throwing the occasional one back. Something flounder-like had this lucky escape, after a long study, the boy smiling at Renee's and my obvious relief that at least one sea creature got to live to swim another day. A blackened cooking pot and gas cylinder contraption (lit blithely by the youngest boy) provided tea and coffee, and later in the day a big fat fried fish each for me and Renee, and lots of little fish for the fishermen (no doubt the nonsalable ones) for lunch. It was the best fish I had ever tasted.

During the day we had been alternating with the captain on the VHF radio, liaising with the other English speakers, and eventually the *Free Gaza* had to call a halt to things because of limited fuel. Our fishermen were loathe to leave and lagged behind fishing as they went, eventually stopping altogether when some problem happened with the nets.

Our captain radioed for the others to leave without us, and we hung about while they began fixing the problem. To our great joy, Renee and I understood we could swim. Completely out of sight of land in any direction, we leapt into the gleaming Gaza Sea. Our boat maneuvered itself a short distance from us in a slightly worrying manner (swimming in long sleeves and long trousers isn't easy) but stopped after a bit, so we caught up, and they hauled us back in. As I sat on the rug on the bow drip-drying, drinking my first lusciously sweet and minty Palestinian tea in three years, I couldn't have been happier.

While all this had been happening, two Israeli ships packed up and went home, and one lurked on the horizon in a slightly bored manner. As soon as we set off however, it took off after us, catching up at an alarming rate. Our captain asked us to radio the *Free Gaza* to come back for us. As soon as this was agreed, the Israeli ship stopped. We radioed them back, "Don't worry. Ship stopped. Don't come." At which the Israeli ship began again to advance. We radioed again, and again it stopped. We began to catch onto the game when this was repeated a third time. Finally the military decided to do what initially looked like an attack but turned out to be just making some sort of point—the grey torpedo-like vessel came full speed toward us, circled us once as close as it could so that our boat would be rocked by its heavy wake, then resumed following us from a distance.

So Renee and I, our bellies full of fish and our bodies covered in salt, settled back on the deck with my iPod. The shuffler provided a soundtrack of Blondie's "Maria," Ani di Franco's "Not a Pretty Girl," Billy Bragg's "Internationale," Nancy Kerr and James Fagan's "Tiller Song," and Crowded House's "Don't Dream It's Over." Occasionally one of us would open an eye, squint toward the Israeli ship, announce, "Nope—guns still not pointing at us. That's nice."

"Best catch in four years," our captain said wistfully, as we headed toward the shore. Finally we caught up with the other boats, which were waiting to arrive in port with us. As we pulled in, we watched all the seasick sunburnt journalists being helped off the *Free Gaza*. Vik waved at us from the deck, shouting "Free Gaza... two and Israel... zero!"

Lauren Booth, August 26

The most common metaphor used to describe life for the 1.5 million inhabitants of the Gaza Strip in Palestine is that of a prison. But I am able to report conclusively that this metaphor is inaccurate. I appeal to those with an interest in honest reporting to stop using this term to describe conditions here. For Gaza, besides having fixed parameters patrolled by armed forces, has little in common with a prison. For a start,

175

prisoners in Europe receive three meals a day. While the taste and quality of these meals varies, each day's food allowance is nutritionally balanced to ensure prisoners receive the optimum vitamins and minerals appropriate for their age group. No one goes hungry in a British jail.

Palestinians in Gaza are eating less. Parents are forced by the ever-tightening Israeli restrictions at the border, forcing them to reduce their children's daily intake merely to ensure that they can survive day by day. A study by the World Food Programme and UNRWA in May of 2008 found that 89 percent of the surveyed population had reduced the quality of food they have bought, while 75 percent had reduced the quantity they ate since January 2008. The food that packs the shelves here is largely made up of biscuits, sweets, crisps, and fizzy drinks—empty carbs, sugar, and fat- laden junk.

Local medical experts report that in Gaza, a diabetes time bomb is about to explode as a result of the siege. Almost all families have reduced their consumption of fresh fruit and vegetables to save money and very few Palestinians now eat fresh (red) meat. Families cannot afford to compensate for the lack of protein and vitamins. Considering the high prevalence of anaemia and other micronutrient deficiencies, this will have health consequences in the long term, especially for children.

I walked through Beach Camp, the refugee camp where Ismail Haniyeh, the prime minister, lives with his family. We were immediately surrounded by many of the camp's curious children. Many of the children's eyes seemed oddly flat and dull; a milky mist covers the cornea in many cases. Dr. Khamis El Essi, a rehabilitation specialist, randomly inspected the skin, teeth, and eyes of the barefoot children crowding around us on the muddy paths running between their impoverished homes.

"This boy's eyes are dull—lack of minerals," he said of one eight-year-old boy. Another child, whom I estimated to be roughly the same as my eldest daughter Alex (seven), was smiling at us and waving "hello." His mouth revealed five or

176

more partially formed uneven stumps. I presumed his milk teeth had just fallen out. After a brief interview with the boy, Dr. Khamis told me, "This boy is small for his age. He is twelve. The lack of vitamins in his diet has affected his bones. His poor diet has already ruined his teeth." Signs were clearly visible in all the children of varying degrees of anaemia, poor growth, and malnutrition.

One of my first invitations was to meet the Hamas prime minister, Ismail Haniyeh. A group of us had been asked to lunch at his home, an apartment in the heart of a refugee camp. The entrance to the dining area is unpaved and . There are pools of muddy water, which I had to step through to get to the door.

Haniyeh is a giant of a man but with a "Hey guys, trust me," demeanor that disarms his critics; he's the Tony Blair of Hamas. After we had eaten, we walked the tight, rubbish-strewn alleyways of the refugee camp. There were skinny children everywhere making games out of the trash lying around. The main one seemed to entail crouching in the dirt and donkey dung, and flicking stones at tin cans.

Israel has now restricted entry of food items like fruit, milk and other dairy products, wheat, flour, rice, sugar, salt, cooking oil, and frozen foods. All the key elements of vulnerability in the population have their roots in the military and administrative measures imposed by the Israeli occupation.

This is no natural disaster. This is deliberate man-made malnutrition.

Gazans are faced with regimented border closures and the destruction of assets, such as acres of orchards, like in the town of Beit Hanoun and many other communities. This rationing of imported food supplies, and destruction of domestic food production has lead to soaring food prices, falling incomes and growing unemployment; elements which combine to jeopardize the livelihoods of Palestinians, leading to heavy debt and changes in family eating habits. Previously self-reliant

177

families are falling into the poverty trap: unable to escape from their situation.

I repeat, Gaza is not a prison. It is much more than that.

Yesterday, I met with Dr. Basem N. Naim, the minister of Health in Gaza. His office was experiencing a black out, and there was no lighting. We sat in dimness to talk about the current situation for hospitals and patients.

With the international refusal of governments to cooperate with Hamas, even on' social issues such as health and education, it is impossible for the ministry of health to have any forward planning for patient care. Dr. Basem gave the example of many cancer patients who receive the first two treatments for their life threatening condition. When the date for the third treatment arrives, the drugs are unavailable. Their condition worsens. At some unknown stage in the future, treatment will have to recommence from the start.

Gaza is no prison. Prisoners in the UK receive high quality health care as needed. In a prison, the inmates have access to clean water, good, clean sanitation, and a twenty-four/seven supply of electricity. Here in Gaza, electricity, fuel, and gas have been drastically reduced and are now intermittently cut off due to a lack of fuel. Things are bad here and getting worse.

The fuel situation is a catastrophe. Power is in short supply, affecting hospitals, fresh water availability, sanitation, and the functioning of daily life here under conditions of extreme duress. I have visited hovels in Beach Camp, whose paltry stoves can no longer be used to prepare a single hot meal each day for families of ten and more, who are confined together in very small spaces.

There is no access to fuel. Wood is in sparse supply in this increasingly dusty, barren land, yet increasingly open fires are the only available method of cooking for the mothers of Gaza. Shops are short of everything, and even basic materials have spotty availability. Banned items that are hard to find here but available in western prisons include: clothing, books, computers, telephones, and even shoes.

During our meeting with John Ging (the director of UNRWA), the difficulties faced by aid agencies in getting the raw materials of life through the checkpoints that handle cargo were outlined. For example, it has taken UNRWA many months of wrangling with the Israeli authorities in order to have paper, needed to print books for the agency's many schools, allowed through. The unwarranted, unreasonable delays meant tens of thousands of Gaza's school children faced the 2009 school year without essential textbooks.

Gaza is not a prison. Families (including spouses) are cut off from one another for unlimited periods of time. Life here is one of relentless interruption after another. I attended a candlelit vigil in the Gardens of the Unknown Soldier in Gaza City. This ceremony was held by mothers who had been separated by the IOF from their families in the West Bank and also abroad, and are unable to reach their children because of the siege.

Nisreen is twenty-seven, a stunning beauty with a quiet grace. Candle shaking in her hand, she could hardly restrain her emotional pain as she told me her story. In 2006 she went on a visit from her home in the West Bank town of Qalqilya to relatives in a neighboring village. On her return, a temporary Israeli checkpoint blocked her route home. Born in Gaza, her papers for Qalqilya were ignored; her permit to live there disregarded. Her place of birth was Gaza, and the Israeli guards insisted that back to Gaza she must return. She was driven, crying for mercy, to Erez, accompanied by a female IOF soldier who spoke no Arabic. "I was roughly forced to cross Erez," she told me, "then left here to rot." Nisreen has seen neither her ten-year-old nor her three-year-old son for "fourteen months and two days."

Just this morning my good friend Dr. Mona El Farra, a highly respected physician and author of the award-winning

179

blog, *From Gaza with Love*, was shaking after a call from her sixteen-year-old daughter. Sondos has been visiting family in Jordan; her school year started this week here in Gaza, but for two weeks, permission for her return home to her mother has been confounded and refused without explanation by Israel's border authority.

Family unification has been denied further after the Israeli Knesset passed the Nationality and Entry into Israel Law (July 2003). This bars Palestinians in the occupied territories with an Israeli spouse from getting citizenship or residency status in Israel. The net result is that these families are not allowed to live together.

Thousands of married couples and their children are forced to remain apart, or leave both Israel and the occupied territories, and move abroad. The new law solely targets Palestinians. Besides this law, Israeli Arabs married to Gazans are barred from entering Gaza to visit their families. Meanwhile, Jewish prisoners in Israel are permitted conjugal visits from spouses under law. Wives regularly get pregnant during these 'compassionate' visits. Prisoners around the world may have regular contact with friends and relatives.

The most psychologically punishing element of all under this cruel siege is that Palestinians in Gaza have no idea and certainly no say in when it will end. In a prison, inmates have a fixed release date they can look forward to, a time in the near (or distant) future when they know they will be reunited with loved ones. The people I have met, since arriving here with the Free Gaza Boats are denied this hope. They live devoid of self-determination, adrift from the rest of the world on a sea of imposed uncertainty. In short, they dare not hope at all.

Gaza is not a prison. Someone who is imprisoned is closely confined as a punishment for a crime after due process of law.

Is this a concentration camp? This definition of an enclosed space where innocent victims (usually of one race and including children held against their will) collectively suffer punishment because of their ethnicity or creed is one that should be familiar to every Israeli soldier, politician, and citizen.

For Palestinians in Gaza, a UK prison with access visits from family members, three square meals a day, rehabilitation, and education programs, good sanitary conditions, and health care would be an improvement over life here.

Gaza 2008 is not a prison but it is slowly becoming the largest concentration camp in history.

Dr. Bill, August 27

Some would say the limited cargo we could bring on two small Greek fishing boats that sailed to Gaza was largely symbolic, a drop in the bucket in terms of Gaza's greater needs. This is certainly true in terms of the overwhelming humanitarian needs being deliberately denied to 1.5 million human beings. But for over a hundred young children at the Atfaluna Society for the Deaf in Gaza City, our mission will make a world of difference: the gift of hearing, about how many hearing aids we brought.

Mona El Farra, Edith Lutz, Kathleen Wang, and Bill Dienst are delivering the hearing aids

They were gifts donated by the California-based Palestine Children's Welfare Fund. Such high-tech devices have been deemed a security threat to the state of Israel. So many Gaza children have been denied the ability to hear.

There are hundreds of Gaza's children who are deaf because of the usual congenital causes and to infections. But there are also many who suffer hearing loss because of acute severe noise exposure. There are bombs and artillery shells. And then there are loud explosions due to low altitude sonic booms from Israeli fighter jets that have flown immediately overhead in efforts to collectively scare the population. It is always much easier to devastate than to heal. There are children in Gaza who will spend years suffering the consequences of some reckless Israeli F-16 fighter pilot's joyride.

For the surgical crew at Al Awda Hospital in Jabalya, our mission will mean that several necessary operations can now proceed thanks to new stocks of anesthetic supplies that have been in short supply. For patients who use a clinic in Beit Hanoun, they will now be able to get an electrocardiogram in their own clinic instead of having to travel to the hospital. This is courtesy of some benevolent physicians in Greece who financed two machines. A second ECG machine will be delivered to another small clinic in need. These are only a few small gestures in the greater scheme of things, yes. But they produce tangible results for a few in need. But more importantly, we have opened up a route. In subsequent voyages, future Free Gaza movement boats will bring larger quantities of medical supplies and other cargo ashore.

Our delegation visits factories whose production has been curtailed and in some cases, shut down because essential supplies critical to ongoing factory operations have been blocked. Now the unemployment rate hovers at over 45 percent for the entire Gaza Strip. In some of the refugee camps, the unemployment rate is over 80 percent.

We participate in a peaceful demonstration in Gaza City on behalf of agricultural workers who are equally devastated. Peaceful, direct action like this has a long tradition here in Gaza and other parts of Palestine. If Israel and the West were really serious about wanting to stop what they call "terrorism," one would think that they would respond positively to peaceful demonstrations that call attention to abuses of fundamental human needs.

Most of Gaza's limited agricultural land lies along the border with Israel. In the agricultural community of Beit Hanoun, for example, over 60 percent of the olive and citrus groves in the area have been ripped out by Israeli militarized bulldozers and tanks. The Israeli's claim that this wanton destruction is necessary for their security, since Qassam missiles have sometimes been fired from these orchards. Israel's security always comes at the expense of Gaza's security. It is hard to see how this bizarre and lopsided "security arrangement" can lead to anyone's long-term wellbeing and safety.

We march with hundreds during their weekly demonstration up to the gates of the UNESCO office. The gates are locked shut and no one answers the door. The local UN agencies can do nothing to help the locals other than to voice the plight of these farmers to the UN general assembly. The UN Security Council and its five permanent members dominate the general assembly. Efforts to respond to Israel's cruel policies are vetoed continuously by its chief enabler, the United States.

We also participate in the weekly demonstration with families of prisoners who are held by Israel. They hold pictures of their loved ones. Some have been imprisoned for more than ten years without due process. There are over 10,000 Palestinian prisoners languishing in Israeli jails. These family members protest nonviolently here in Gaza City every week demanding to be heard. When will the outside world ever listen?

Next, our bus, filled with Free Gaza movement passengers and local Palestinians from our host groups, heads south toward the city of Rafah, which borders Egypt. We want to get an assessment of the current situation there.

There is no way of telling by casual observation, but this main north-south road, Salah Al-Din, is a part of one of the oldest thoroughfares in human history. It has been called different names over the millennia, but it also has been a part of the main highway that follows the coast between Morocco and Turkey for over 5,000 years. Unfortunately right now, it is virtually impossible for Gaza's local citizens to travel any further than the forty kilometers between Beit Hanoun in the north and Rafah in the south. The Israelis, and 'applied political pressure through the Americans over the Egyptians', have the local people living alongside this main arterial of the millennia clogged, and sealed off from the rest of the world.

En route we make a stop at Nuseirat Refugee Camp about halfway down the Gaza Strip. Nuseirat is one of four middle camps. The others are Bureij, Maghazi, and finally Deir al Balah, right next to the town of Deir Al Balah, which carries the same name. Before these four camps' creation in 1948, the area was farmland, and there still exists a wee bit of farmland in the limited spaces between the four camps. These four middle camps now collectively comprise a population of over 132,000. And these are the smaller four of the eight refugee camps in Gaza. Jabalya Camp north of Gaza City has 107 thousand people. Beach Camp has around 81 thousand. Rafah Camp has over 97 thousand, and Khan Younis Camp nearly 62 thousand inhabitants. The populations of these camps do not include the larger cities and smaller towns that surround them.

What distinguishes refugee camps in Gaza from the towns that often carry the same name is that the camps are essentially devoid of open land. People are packed into these camps like sardines. Families are crowded together in cinderblock apartments with the roof left incomplete. This has become a classic feature of modern Gaza architecture. The top floor is left undone with rebar pilings for future construction of higher floors to house more people when there are future generations. There is no room to build outward, only upward. The camp population keeps growing.

At the Nuseirat Children's Center, teenage students perform traditional Palestinian Dabke dancing for us. This is an art form that developed before 1948 in more spacious Palestinian villages north of Gaza before the Catastrophe, or *Nakba*, put them in this overcrowded situation. The great-grandparents of today's dancers come from these villages; before they were forced into these camps by the creation of Israel. Many of these former Palestinian villages are now destroyed. Now the memories of theses villages are preserved through dances like the Dabke in refugee camps like Nuseirat.

We head further south, past the rubble of the former Abu Holi checkpoint, which was finally destroyed in September 2005, along with two adjacent former Israeli illegal settlements. Before August 2005, there were about 8,000 Israeli squatters in Gaza. These settlements, along with the various Israeli-only bypass roads and military bases that supported them, controlled about 40 percent of the Gaza Strip and made it off-limits to local Palestinians. These restrictions included about a third of the Gaza beachfront, the former Gush Kativ block of settlements. Once again, the security and safety of 8,000 Israeli settlers came at the expense of over 1.5 million Palestinians confined in Gaza.

The next major city to the south is Khan Younis, which means Jonah's inn in Arabic. It was founded in the fourteenth century as a way station to protect caravans, pilgrims and other travelers who plied this main route. Today it has nearly 200,000 inhabitants, including its adjacent refugee camp. And finally we get to Rafah, which has been in existence since at least 1300 BC. It has a current population of 130 thousand people, of which 84 thousand live in refugee camps. Before 1979 when the Sinai Peninsula was given back to Egypt as part of the Camp David Peace Accords negotiated between Carter, Sadat, and Begin, there had been no distinct border here..

During the late 1990s, the Israeli military authorities tried even harder to disconnect Rafah from the outside world. They built an iron wall to separate Egyptian from Gaza Rafah. The local residents responded by building tunnels. The ruthlessness of the Israeli occupation authorities then became even more apparent. Between 2002 and 2005, they destroyed over 2500 homes and made 20,000 Palestinians homeless in the occupied Palestinian territories. Two thirds of these home demolitions occurred in Rafah, and about 10 percent of Gaza Rafah's entire population was made homeless. The Israeli occupation authorities claim that they uncovered about ninety tunnels in this way. The no man's land was widened to 300 meters, and the area was given the Orwellian misnomer Philadelphi Corridor—brotherly love! It has been anything but.

It is now August 2008. Our FG delegation bus drives right up and over the line where the iron wall used to stand to the new stonewall with Egypt, where we file out. There are still a few piles and fragments of iron wall strewn about that the Hamas authorities have not yet removed. Now the locals can stroll right up to the stonewall on the Egyptian line and shout, "Ahlan-Wa-Sahlan!"(WELCOME) to the Egyptian guards sitting in their towers on the other side. Compared to the Israelis, the Egyptian soldiers are less likely to shoot.

We head back up to Khan Younis to the city offices and meet the mayor. We journey to the West up against where refugees from Khan Younis camp used to try to exist alongside the Gush Kativ block of settlements. These settlements denied locals access to the sea for so many years.

Now they can travel to the sea without being sniped at. But now the new land acquired from the former settlement is on the brink of a catastrophic, occupation-caused environmental disaster that could be easily prevented. Because of extreme rationing by the Israeli occupation authorities of fuel to the area, the local sewage treatment plant is limited in how much sewage it can process. Consequently, a huge cesspool is building up west of Khan Younis. This cesspool lies up the hill from perhaps the most beautiful beach in Gaza, which was formerly a part of the illegal Gush Kativ settlement block.

The water tables here have been among the best in Gaza; hence the location of this former settlement. Palestinians now have access to this area again. We visit this beach, and some of us swim in its crystal-clear, aquamarine waters. It is still beautiful. Only problem is that if the cesspool uphill keeps building up without proper processing of sewage, it could rupture and contaminate the delicate high-quality water table below it and spoil the adjacent beach and coastline.

Our bus heads back toward Gaza City via the coastal road, formerly reserved for illegal Israeli settlers only and off-limits to Palestinians for many years. There is abundant vegetation; this is probably the most scenic area in the Gaza Strip. Musheir El Farra is from these parts. He was born and raised in Khan Younis but now lives in Sheffield, England, where he is a civil engineer and Palestinian rights activist. His family has property around here and his two sisters, who are both physicians, have been among our hosts here in Gaza.

Chapter 10: Gaza on My Mind

Jeff Halper, Bill Dienst, Greta Berlin, Sharyn Lock

On August 26, Jeff Halper decided to leave through the Erez crossing back to Israel. He was going to challenge Israel's right to close borders on the Palestinians and those who supported them and not let them pass. As he arrived on the Israeli side, he was arrested and thrown into prison. The Israeli media covered his arrest and also reported that the reason Israel 'let us through to Gaza' was that we would be deprived of any publicity. How wrong they were.

Jeff Halper

Now, a few days after my release from jail in the wake of my trip to Gaza, I'm posting a few notes to sum things up.

First, the mission of the Free Gaza movement to break the Israeli siege proved a success beyond all expectations. Our reaching Gaza and leaving has created a free and regular channel between Gaza and the outside world. It has done so because it has forced the Israeli government to make a clear policy declaration: that it is not occupying Gaza and therefore will not prevent the free movement of Palestinians in and out (at least by sea).

Israel's security concerns can easily be accommodated by instituting a technical system of checks similar to those of other ports. Any attempt on the part of Israel to backtrack on this by preventing ships in the future from entering or leaving Gaza with goods and passengers, including Palestinians, may be immediately interpreted as an assertion of control, and therefore of occupation, opening Israel to accountability for war crimes under international law, something Israel tries to avoid at all costs.

188

Gone is the obfuscation that has allowed Israel to maintain its control of the occupied territories without assuming any responsibility: from now on, Israel is either an occupying power accountable for its actions and policies, or Palestinians have every right to enjoy their human right of traveling freely in and out of their country. Israel can no longer have it both ways. Not only did our two little boats force the Israel military and government to give way, but they also changed fundamentally the status of Israel's control of Gaza.

When we finally arrived in Gaza after a day and a half sail, the welcome we received from 40,000 joyous Gazans was overwhelming and moving. People sought me out in particular; eager it seemed to speak Hebrew with an Israeli after years of isolation from Israel. The message I received by people of all factions during my three days there was the same: How do we (we in the sense of all of us living in their country not just Palestinians or Israelis) get out of this mess? Where are we going? The discourse was not even political: what is the solution: one state or two? It was just common sense and straightforward, based on the assumption that we will all continue living in the same country and this stupid conflict, with its walls and siege and violence, is bad for everybody. "Don't Israelis see that?" people would ask me.

The answer, unfortunately, is "no." To be honest, we Israeli Jews are the problem. The Palestinians years ago accepted our existence in the country as a people and are willing to accept ANY solution. It is us who want exclusivity over the land of Israel; it is us who cannot conceive of a single country, who cannot accept the national presence of Palestinians (we talk about "Arabs" in our country), and who have eliminated by our settlements even the possibility of the two-state solution in which we take 80 percent of the land.

So it's sad, truly sad, that our "enemies" want peace and coexistence (and tell me that in HEBREW), and we don't. Yeah, we Israeli Jews want "peace," but in the meantime what

189

we have—almost no attacks, a feeling of security, a "disappeared" Palestinian people, a booming economy, tourism, and ever-improving international status—seems just fine. If "peace" means giving up settlements, land and control, why do it? What's wrong with the status quo?

When in Gaza I also managed to see old friends, especially Eyad al-Sarraj of the Gaza Community Mental Health Programme and Raja Sourani, director of the Palestinian Center for Human Rights, whom I visited in his office. I also received honorary Palestinian citizenship, including a passport, which was very meaningful to me as an Israeli Jew. When I was in Gaza, everyone in Israel, including the media who interviewed me, warned me to be careful: to watch out for my life. They asked me if I was scared.

Well, the only time I felt genuine and palpable fear during the entire journey was when I got back to Israel. I went from Gaza through the Erez checkpoint because I wanted to make the point that the siege is not only by sea. On the Israeli side I was immediately arrested, charged with violating a military order prohibiting Israelis from being in Gaza, and jailed at the Shikma prison in Ashkelon.

In my cell that night, someone recognized me from the news. All night, rightwing Israelis physically threatened me, and I was sure I wouldn't make it till the morning. Ironically, there were three Palestinians in my cell who kind of protected me, so the danger was from Israelis, not Palestinians, in Gaza as well as in Israel. (One Palestinian from Hebron was in jail for being illegally in Israel; I was in jail for being illegally in Palestine.) As it stands, I'm out on bail. The state will probably press charges in the next few weeks and I could be jailed for two or so months.

I now am a Palestinian in every sense of the word: On Monday I received my Palestinian citizenship, and on Tuesday I was already in an Israeli jail.

Though the operation was a complete success, the siege will only be genuinely if we keep up the movement in and out of Gaza. The boats are scheduled to return in two to four weeks, and I am now working on getting a boatload of Israelis. My only frustration with what was undoubtedly a successful operation was with the fact that Israelis just don't get it and don't want to get it. The implications of our being the strong party and the fact that the Palestinians are the ones truly seeking peace are too threatening to their hegemony and self-perceived innocence.

What I encountered in perhaps a dozen interviews, and what I read about myself and our trip written by "journalists" who never even attempted to speak to me or the others, was a collective image of Gaza, the Palestinians and our interminable conflict that could only be described as fantasy. Rather than inquire about my experiences, motives, or views, my interviewers, especially on the mainstream radio, spent their time forcing their slogans and uniformed prejudices on me. It was as if giving me a space to explain myself might deal a death-blow to their tightly-held conceptions.

Ben Dror Yemini of the popular Ma'ariv newspaper called us a "satanic cult." Another suggested that a prominent contributor to the Free Gaza movement was a Palestinian-American who had been questioned by the FBI, as if that had to do with anything (the innuendo being we were supported, perhaps even manipulated or worse, by "terrorists").

Others were more explicit: Wasn't it true that we were giving Hamas a PR victory? Why was I siding with Palestinian fishermen-gun smugglers against my own country, which sought only to protect its citizens? Some simply yelled at me, like an interviewer on Arutz 99. And when all else failed, my interlocutors could always fall back on good old cynicism: "Peace is impossible. Jews and Arabs are different species. You can't trust them." Or bald assertions: "They just want to destroy us." Then there's the paternalism: "Well, I guess it's good to have a few idealists like you around..."

Nowhere in the many interviews was there a genuine curiosity about what I was doing or what life was like in Gaza. No one was interested in a different perspective, especially if it challenged his cherished slogans. No one was going beyond the old, tired slogans. Plenty of reference, though, to terrorism, Qassam missiles, and Palestinian snubbing our valiant efforts to make peace and none whatsoever to occupation, house demolitions, siege, land expropriation, or settlement expansion, not to mention the killing, imprisonment, and impoverishment of their civilian population. As if we had nothing to do with the conflict, as if we were just living our normal, innocent lives and bad people decided to throw Qassam rockets at us.

Above all, there is no sense of our responsibility or any willingness to accept responsibility for the ongoing violence and conflict. Instead just a thoughtless, automatic appeal to an image of Gaza and "Arabs" (we don't generally use the term "Palestinians") that is diametrically opposed to what I've seen and experienced: a slavish repeating of mindless (and wrong) slogans that serve only to eliminate any possibility of truly grasping the situation. In short, a fantasy Gaza as perceived from within a bubble carefully constructed so as to deflect any uncomfortable reality.

The greatest insight this trip has given me is understanding why Israelis don't get it: a media composed of people who should know better but who possess little critical ability and feel more comfortable inside a box created by self-serving politicians than in trying to do something far more creative: understanding what in the hell is going on here. Still, I formulated clearly my messages to my fellow Israelis and that constitutes the main content of my interviews and talks:

1. Despite what our political leaders say, there is a political solution to the conflict and there are partners for peace. If anything, we of the peace movement must not allow the

powers that be to mystify the conflict: to present it as a "clash of civilizations." The Israeli-Palestinian conflict is political and, as such, it has a political solution.

2. The Palestinians are not our enemies. In fact, I urge my fellow Israeli Jews to disassociate from the dead-end politics of our failed political leaders by declaring, in concert with Israeli and Palestinian peacemakers: We refuse to be enemies.

3. As the infinitely stronger party in the conflict and the only occupying power, we Israelis must accept responsibility for our failed and oppressive policies. Only we can end the conflict.

Dr. Bill, August 27-28

This morning, I along with Takis Politis, a university professor of information technology at the University of Tsessalia in Volos, Greece, and Tasos Kourakis, a Greek MP and also a podiatrist and professor of genetics at University of Aristoteles in Salonica, head out separately from the others on our FG delegation. Dr. Khamis El-Essi takes us to the Islamic University in Gaza City. Its campus is right next to the more secular University of Al Azhar, which has more affiliations with Fateh, while the Islamic University tends to favor Hamas. I have visited Al Azhar University before. It has a pharmacy and medical school. So does the Islamic University.

Based on their respective affiliations, there was armed conflict between students of these universities in the summer of 2007. There is still some evidence of damage and graffiti on the buildings here at the Islamic University, stemming from the June 2007 internecine warfare, but most of it has now been repaired. The campus is otherwise quite attractive, with modern buildings alongside mosques with tall minarets.

We are taken to the office of Professor Kamel Sha'ek, the president of the Islamic University. Professor Sha'ek did his undergraduate work at Cairo University in Egypt. He then

193

received postgraduate degrees in construction management at Colorado State University and also in the UK and Spain.

Before 1967, there were no universities in the West Bank and Gaza Strip. At that time, students had easy access to universities in Jordan, Egypt, and the outside world. After the Israeli occupation in 1967, coming and going from Gaza became more difficult. Universities in the West Bank were successfully established in Hebron, Bethlehem, Birzeit, and later in Abu Dis, east of Jerusalem.

In Gaza, the Islamic University was the first university to be established in 1978, nine years after the occupation began. Al Azhar University was then established in 1992. According to Professor Sha'ek, the Islamic University's enrollment is currently 60 percent female and 40 percent male. They have hosted exchange students from other countries in the past, but this has become more difficult with the illegal siege.

We are taken to an information technology lecture hall, which has state-of-the-art computer terminals at each desk. Later, we visit the molecular genetics lab and then the anatomy lab, with modern three dimensional anatomy models, which can be viewed in cross sections. Computerized virtual anatomy lesions are viewed on computer terminals instead of cadaver dissections. We meet briefly with about twenty-one female second-year medical students who are all dressed conservatively.

We depart the Islamic University and Dr. Khamis drives us in his small economy car, which has been converted to burn propane instead of petroleum. Propane is currently in greater supply and therefore less expensive because of the siege.

There are also "falafel mobiles" driving around Gaza, which burn vegetable oil and other biodiesel products. The siege has made the local population very creative and innovative.

We arrive at Al Wafa' Rehabilitation Hospital on the northeastern margins of the Gaza Strip, about a half kilometer from the barrier with Israel. We head upstairs to the main

194

nurses station. On the wall there are pictures of two male nurses who are now martyrs. But these martyrs were not involved in any sort of armed conflict. They were simply trying to do their job as nurses.

On February 7, 2003, the area where Wafa' Hospital is located was under an incursion by IOF. These two nurses were moving patients upstairs on the men's coma ward. They both were shot and killed by a single bullet fired through the window by an Israeli sniper, who was perched on the top of the adjacent building immediately to the east of Al Wafa' Hospital. You can still see where the lone bullet penetrated through the glass here on the coma ward. The IOF claimed that they did not know this was a hospital, yet there is clearly a white flag with a red crescent posted on the northeast corner of the hospital, and "Al Wafa' Rehabilitation Hospital" clearly written on the eastern side of the building in Arabic and English (but not Hebrew).

We tour wards full of people with shattered lives who have been forgotten by the outside world, but not by Al Wafa' Hospital: A school teacher who was shot in the head and survived in a persistent vegetative state; a man shot through the spinal cord and now permanently paralyzed. We also see genetic cases that produce orthopedic disabilities, like three girls from the same family who need specialized attention in order to walk. Because of the isolation in Gaza combined with traditional clanship, there are frequent marriages between distant cousins, and thus relatively high genetic diseases here.

The sun deliquesces into the sea on the final night before the FG boats are ready to set sail back to Cyprus. Our hosts in the Popular Committee to End the Siege have a big gathering in the Legislative Council building to send us off. The sun rises.

Ten of the original international passengers who arrived five days ago on the boats have decided to stay, including me. Four of us plan to leave through Rafah this weekend, and six

195

others plan to stay on for longer periods of time and do solidarity work here.

Before departure, we have a final gathering on the veranda at Al Deira Hotel. We each are awarded Palestinian citizenship, including a brand new Palestinian Authority VIP passport!

Leaving with the Free Gaza Boats are local Palestinians from Gaza who have been unable to get out by other means. These include a family, a woman separated from her husband, and Saed, a boy, with a high-level amputation suffered from an Israeli mortar shell, seeking specialty care abroad.

Taking wounded Saed back to Cyprus for treatment aboard the Liberty. Nikolas Bolos shows him the huge fish caught on board the boat.

It is getting time for the boats to leave. So we head down to the marina by bus. It takes time to prepare the boats for casting

196

off. There is both happiness and melancholy as Palestinian passengers say good-bye to their families on shore, not knowing if or when they will be able to return to Gaza. It is getting later in the day. The boats' departure is behind schedule and there is growing anxiety that there is limited daylight. It would be best if the boats were able to make it out into international waters before the sun sets, just in case they have any run-ins with the Israeli Navy. Finally, the boats pull out from the marina at 3:30 P.M. With top speeds at just over six nautical miles, this leaves just enough time to get out beyond the twenty-mile limit before nightfall.

A half hour later, the fishing vessels turn around toward shore, and we can see four Israeli warships closing in from the north and south around the FG boats. At sunset, we are relieved to receive word that our vessels have made it out into international waters without any direct interference from the Israeli Navy, only intimidation.

Sharyn: Newsflash! Boats Back, Friday, August 29

The *Free Gaza* and the *Liberty* are arriving back at Cyprus any minute now, safe from their return journey that began yesterday. They are carrying seven Palestinian passengers who (according to the requirements of the Cyprus authorities) have valid visas or second passports, yet physically could not leave Gaza because of the siege.

I'm still here with nine others. We had an action today at Erez border accompanying a female patient named Majdeya to the crossing in face of threatened fire if we proceeded. She's been trying for seven months to get to her scheduled operation in an East Jerusalem hospital to have a spinal tumour removed. Didn't get her in, but did get a "promise" of "by Sunday when her current operation is due" and didn't get shot either which was nice. (I do wish people wouldn't sing things like "We shall

197

overcome" during what might be our final moments though, especially out of tune)

The article below from the Israeli press is interesting, particularly because of the official comments . . . there really is potential to sail again in a few weeks, if ONLY we can get some big donors to cover our debts so we don't have to sell the boats to do it that way:

Israel allowed two boats carrying international activists and seven Palestinians to leave Gaza on Thursday and sail without interruption back to Cyprus.

The boats had been allowed to dock in Gaza harbor last Saturday after the government decided not to clash with the 44 human rights activists aboard and play into what officials said was a clear provocation intended to damage Israel's public image.

The Free Gaza movement said that among the Palestinians who left Gaza were five children, including 10-year-old Saed Mosleh from Beit Hanoun, who the group said had lost one of his legs to an Israeli tank shell. He left Gaza with his father to seek medical treatment abroad. Also on board was the Darwish family, who will be reunited with its relatives in Cyprus.

"I can't believe we're finally able to leave for medical treatment," said Khaled Mosleh, Saed's father. "This is a miracle of God."

Out of the 44 activists who arrived on Saturday, ten will remain in Gaza to do long-term monitoring, the movement said.

The Free Gaza movement plans to return to Gaza with another delegation in the near future and to ask the United Nations, the Arab League and other international organizations to organize similar sea-based operations.

Israeli defense officials said Thursday that there was no set policy on how Israel would react in the event that another ship coming from international waters tries to enter Gaza. Officials said that as of now, Israel knows of no plans for other boats to set sail for Gaza, and that if other boats did try to enter, Israel would decide how to handle the situation on a case-by-case basis.

"Each case will be examined individually," one official said.

In Thursday's case, the official said Israel had been aware of who was on board the ships - including the identity of the Palestinians - and had not interfered since none of the passengers posed a security risk.

"None of the passengers was dangerous to Israel, and they were not coming into Israel, so there was no reason to stop them," the official said. "If a boat, however, tried to take wanted Hamas terrorists out of Gaza, that would be a different story."

Greta, arriving in Cyprus, August 29

We arrived safely last night. The trip home was much less eventful and much less emotional. We pulled out in the early afternoon of August 28 and pointed toward Cyprus. Three hours later, just as we were getting ready to pass the 20-mile limit into international waters, the *Liberty* lost a fan belt. Derek hung over the side of the *Free Gaza* and passed them a new one and our tool box, and we sat there, a mile away from safety, as the men on board the *Liberty* tried to fix the engine. We wanted to be well out to sea by nightfall, and we could see the Israeli navy hovering in the background, watching us; an hour passed and a loud 'huzzah' came from the *Liberty*, and the engine roared back to life.

Ironically, the Israeli news reported the next day that we had stopped as 'a provocation,' against the Israeli navy, wanting them to attack us. If they had only known that, once again, our boats didn't work, and we were sitting out there hoping the damned engine would flip over and start.

On board my boat the *Free Gaza* was a family of Palestinians who had not been let out of the concentration camp called Gaza for five years. The mother had given birth to her youngest son four years ago, and the family, living in Cyprus, had not seen him. The joy on the faces of Hana's family was worth waiting the extra time to leave. We had to make sure that the Cypriot authorities would allow them in.

199

On board the *Liberty* was a ten-year-old boy whose leg had been shot off by the Israeli military. He was from Khan Younis. The story is that he was standing with his friend as an Israeli tank invaded his town. A sniper shot him through one leg, and when he stood to run, the sniper shot him through the other one, causing huge damage to the leg. It was amputated at the hip. Again, we had to wait for Cypriot authorities to give permission for him to transit to another country.

On the first page of the Cyprus Mail is a photo of the boy with Osama, one of our organizers. Even though we came in at 9:00 P.M., the media was all over the quay waiting for us. Although we didn't get seasick this time, many of us, because we are so exhausted, are feeling the land effects today, swaying as we try to walk down the streets.

It has been a week of overriding joy, sadness at the condition of so many sick and wounded Palestinians, hope for the future, and disbelief that we not only arrived safely but left safely. As we pulled out of Gaza yesterday, seven Israeli naval vessels surrounded the Palestinian fishermen who joyfully escorted us six miles out. The last view we had of Gaza was of the seven gunboats surrounding the fishermen. We've heard from our Israeli sources that they arrested four of them.

Saying "good-bye" to us as we sail back to Cyprus, the fishing boats accompany us out of the port, Gaza City in the background.

Chapter 11: Stealing Gaza's Gas
The Real Reason for Illegal Blockade

David K. Schermerhorn

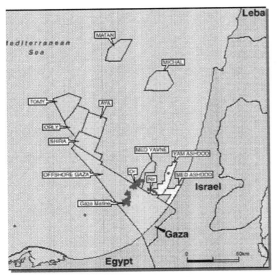

Why should Gaza be so coveted, when Israel says they withdrew their illegal settlers and turned over the territory to the people, and all they have gotten in return are rockets from the 'militants' of Gaza?

Illustration is courtesy of Hebrew Energy Dictionary.

They continuously say they attack the Palestinians in Gaza, because of the security of Israel is at stake. If they are to be believed, it is the Palestinians of Gaza who are the aggressors. So, let's looks briefly at some of the history of this war-torn territory and the real reason Israel continues to commit slow-motion genocide against the people there.

There is an historical connection between the Gaza community and offshore fishery. In recent times, some 3,000 fishermen in over 700 boats made their livelihood in the waters off the shores of Gaza. Before 1978 when the fishing area

202

included the sea off the Sinai coastline, the area covered some 75,000 square kilometers.

The larger boats are about 20 meters in length and usually carry a crew of 7. They are typically trawlers using downriggers to lower their nets to the ocean bed. Currently their main catch is bream or sardines that average between 8 and 14 inches. Smaller craft, hassakas, normally deploy their nets a few hundred meters off shore. The nets are then hauled in by hand. These catches are very modest.

On September 13, 1993, the Oslo Agreement was signed marking the basis for a peaceful accord between Israel and the Palestinians. The GAZA-JERICHO AGREEMENT of 1994 outlined specific steps needed to realize the general provisions of the Oslo Agreement.

Under its terms, the Gaza fishermen were free to use a marine corridor from their shores extending twenty nautical miles bounded by restricted, or border, zones to the north and south abutting Israeli and Egyptian waters.

However, beginning in late 2000, the Israeli military initiated its continuing campaign of intimidation and harassment against fishing boats that ventured near or beyond a six nautical mile limit.[1] Their patrol boats attacked and harassed the fishermen on a daily basis. As of 2010, the Israelis have killed eighteen and wounded over 220 fishermen.

Among the warships used were ones in the Dabur and Dvora classes. Their armaments include 20 mm to 30 mm cannons, machine guns, automatic grenade launchers plus high-pressure water cannons. Some have 700-mile ranges and top speeds of 52 knots. Originally they were built in the US but in recent years they are constructed by Israel Aircraft at a plant in the Negev.

No formal notice or explanation of these restrictions was ever given to the Palestinians, although the year 2000 is very important. Any written regulations have been enforced by Israeli machine guns and water cannons.

Since the Operation Cast Lead "ceasefire" in January 2009, attacks by the Israeli Navy have become more aggressive, often occurring within a few hundred yards of the shore. Even the people of Gaza, walking on their beaches have been wounded by gunfire intended for the fishing boats. The fishermen continue to be killed, wounded, or arrested. Their boats continue to be targeted or impounded. The noose of the illegal blockade grows tighter.

Israeli Attack on Gaza Fishing Boats – Stealing Gaza's Gas

For the first fifty years after Israel's founding, the country explored extensively for natural gas or oil deposits with little success. The old Jewish joke about Moses walking in the desert for 20 years and going to the one country where there was no oil or natural gas seemed to be true. More than 400 onshore and 25 offshore exploratory wells were dug during that period with no success. Nothing major was either on the land or in the territorial waters of Israel. Therefore, Israel was obliged to import 85 percent of its energy needs by buying coal and petroleum products from Egypt, Russia, Mexico and elsewhere.

September 13, 1993: The Oslo Agreement was signed laying the basis for peaceful relations between Israel and the Palestinians.

May 4, 1994: PLO Chairman Yasser Arafat and Israeli Prime Minister Yitzhak Rabin signed the Gaza-Jericho Agreement as part of the subsequent procedure called for in the Oslo Agreement.

In that agreement, Article XI established three maritime activity zones that extended twenty nautical miles out to sea from the coast of Gaza.[2] Two narrow zones running parallel to the boundaries of Egyptian and Israeli waters were designated no fishing areas. Under the terms of the agreement the larger remaining zone "will be open for fishing, recreation, and

204

economic activities." For the next six years the fishermen of Gaza operated freely within the zone with no major confrontations by the Israelis.

In addition the UN Convention on the Law of the Sea, part V, describes an exclusive economic zone (EEZ) that would grant Gaza control of all seabed assets up to 200 nautical miles from its shore.[3] There is speculation that vast deposits of natural gas are located beyond the twenty-mile maritime activity zone. Such a resource would give Gaza the potential of becoming another Dubai in a relatively short period if they were allowed to develop their own deposits.[4]

1999: The British Gas Group (BG Group) discovered a vast deposit of natural gas within Gaza's Maritime Activity Zone: Over 1.4 trillion cubic feet equal to 150 million barrels of oil were estimated to be there. Located about fifteen miles off the coast, the deposits were named Gaza Marine one and two. It was estimated that there were sufficient reserves to generate electric power for all Palestinian needs for a decade and still have a surplus to export.[5]

On November 8, 1999: Chairman Yasser Arafat signed an agreement giving BG Group 90 percent interest with only 10 percent to Consolidated Contractors Company, an Athens-based Palestinian entity connected to the PLO. They and the Palestinian Investment Fund (PIF) had the option to later assume up to 40 percent interest. (A final allocation of the rights continues to be contested between BG Group, Israel, Egypt, and the Palestinians in obscured ongoing negotiations.)

In the late 1990s Noble Energy, based in Houston, Texas, began explorations for natural gas off the Israeli coast in conjunction with Israeli partners Avner Oil and Delek Drilling.

March 2000: Nobel Energy 'announced' the discovery of the Mari-B natural gas deposit located approximately fifteen miles off shore and close to the Gaza marine zones. Initial estimates projected reserves exceeding 1 trillion cubic feet of natural gas.

July 25, 2000: Yasser Arafat walked out on the Camp David meeting over the status of Jerusalem.[6] But others working with the Israelis and Palestinians say that Richard Pearle was the instigator of the conflict, telling Barak that he should walk out instead and wait for a better deal from Bush, when he became the new President. [7]

September 27, 2000: Yasser Arafat traveled 19 miles off the Gaza coast to light the first flare stack flowing up from the natural gas deposit. An Israeli oil consortium had contested the Palestinian rights to the gas, but this suit was overturned in an Israeli court. Original estimates for development and production expenses were in the area of two billion dollars. Profits were estimated at another two billion dollars.

In the initial stages, BG considered running an underwater pipeline twenty miles from Gaza Marine directly to Gaza, where it would be used in retrofitted generators to provide power. Excess gas would be piped to the West Bank or converted to liquid natural gas (LNG) for export to foreign buyers. [8]

This plan was abandoned in early 2000, when Ariel Sharon announced that the Israelis would never buy gas directly from the Palestinians. At that point the BG Group negotiated with Egypt to run an undersea pipeline to a plant at El-Arish, Egypt. The gas would then be piped to Israel so that they would not have to deal directly with the Palestinians.

Under pressure from Tony Blair, BG Group was forced to negotiate with the Israelis, instead, who wanted the pipe to run directly to Ashqelon. Those discussions were so long and contentious that ultimately the BG Group closed their Israel office and again began dealing with Egypt.[9]

September 28, 2000: The day after Arafat lit the first flare stack, Ariel Sharon marched into the Temple Mount despite warnings by Arafat and other leading Palestinians. The predictable riots and deaths following this provocation marked the beginning of the second Intifada. As a result, Sharon was elected prime minister in February 2001.[10] He reaffirmed that Israel would never buy gas from the Palestinians. After the outbreak of the second Intifada, the Israelis began an ever-tightening blockade of Gaza (it had been blockaded since the early 90s) with fewer and fewer trucks allowed in by land and no foreign boats allowed to enter the Gaza port.

Late 2000: Attacks by Israeli patrol boats against Gaza fishing boats began and have continued to this day. These attacks on fishermen started only after the discovery of the natural gas deposits, and five years before Hamas freely won the legislative elections on January 25, 2006.[11]

It is apparent that these assaults on the fishermen had nothing to do with security or with Hamas. Instead it had everything to do with Israel controlling a four billion dollar resource belonging to the Palestinians.

2003: a platform was completed in the Mari-B reserve and gas began flowing through a pipeline to Ashqelon. Until 2009, the Mari-B reserve remained the only sizable reserve found in Israeli territory. Although it was significant, it did not approach meeting Israel's energy needs and was a finite resource.

While there is no hard evidence yet, it appears quite possible for the Israelis to access the gas deposits located in the Gaza marine from the Mari-B platform. Slant drilling techniques now allow bits to reach up to 25,000 feet horizontally from a standing platform.[12]

October 2001: Following the 9/11 attacks, the US State Department included both Hamas and Hezbollah on their terrorist list, although neither one had anything to do with 9/11.

August 2002: In response to a request from Prime Minister Sharon, the secretary-general of the United Nations appointed Ms. Catherine Bertini as his personal humanitarian envoy to assess the humanitarian needs of the Palestinians. At the end of her visit to the area, she made numerous recommendations, including one that dealt with the fishing boats. In her report, she included a list of "Previous Commitments Made by Israel."

Item two states: "The fishing zone for Palestinian fishing boats off the Gaza coast is twelve nautical miles. This policy needs to be fully implemented."[13] But it never was.

Despite Bertini's recommendations, Israeli attacks became more frequent on fishing boats that passed a six-mile limit. Most boats carried a GPS, so they could determine their exact positions. Some captains were intimidated by the Israeli threats and turned back before crossing the no-go line. Others continued to go farther out despite the increased danger of attack.

The consequences to the fishing industry in Gaza are horrific. The fishery closer to shore has collapsed after so many boats were forced to operate in such a limited area. In addition the waters near shore are polluted due to sewage pouring in from sewage pipes. This is one more example of an infrastructure crippled by the Israelis.[14]

Before the siege, Gaza's fishermen caught 3,000 tons of fish each year. Now it is less than 500 tons.

In addition to firing cannons and machine guns at or near the fishing boats, the Israelis periodically introduce noxious chemical substances into the water fired from their boats that leaves a foul odor on any fish or crewmen on deck. It is probable that the chemicals are the same used by the Israelis in crowd control on land. Under the Chemical Weapons Convention of 1997, it is specified, "Each state party undertakes not to use riot control agents as a method of warfare."[15]

On occasion, the patrol boats have purposely rammed into fishing boats, damaging the vessels and endangering the crew. Numerous times, the Israelis have forced fishermen to jump into the water and remain there for up to three hours, until they are exhausted and close to hypothermia.

Periodically, the Israelis impound fishing boats and take them and their crews to Ashdod, Israel or some other port. The crewmen are generally released after being photographed and interrogated. The boats are held for indefinite periods. Captured fishermen report that the Israelis pressure them to become informers in exchange for the freedom to fish. [16]

September 12, 2005: Israel announced that it had ended the occupation of Gaza and withdrew its forces. But it continued to maintain control of air and sea-lanes, as well as all border crossings on land. The amount of vehicular traffic remained extremely limited and never approached a typical pre-occupation daily level. The ability for persons to enter or leave Gaza continued to be restricted. Permission or denial for passage was often arbitrary and unpredictable. The conditions of an occupation continue to prevail.

January 2006: Hamas won 76 of 132 seats in the Palestinian Legislative Council in an open honest election. After a bloody battle with Fatah elements that were supported by both Israeli and US interests, Hamas took control of Gaza. Israel and the United States immediately reiterated that Hamas was a "terrorist organization" and that they would continue to have no public contact with it. The restrictions at the border crossings were tightened further with even more severe limitations on the admission of produce, materials, medicines, and people. Anemia and malnutrition are widespread as a result.

Early June 2008: Israeli Defense Minister Ehud Barak instructed the Israel defense forces to secretly prepare for an invasion of Gaza, later known as Operation Cast Lead.[17]

June 2008: Israel contacted BG Group to propose renewing negotiations over the natural gas deposits in Gaza. Actual negotiations overseen by Ehud Olmert were taking place in October 2008. It appears that Israel wished to reach an agreement with BG Group before the secretly planned invasion began. [18]

June 19, 2008: Hamas and Israel signed a six-month truce agreement calling for cessation of rocket firings by Hamas and military incursions by Israel. In May 2008, over 300 rockets had been fired. Hamas was led to believe that significant increase in shipments would be allowed to enter Gaza; but that never happened.

Before the truce, roughly seventy UN and NGO trucks were allowed to bring provisions into Gaza each day, compared with some 900 permitted before the Israeli clamp down in 2000. Hamas was led to believe that a similar flow of traffic would be restored. Instead, Israel allowed only an increase from the seventy to ninety trucks. [19]

August 23, 2008: Two boats, the *Liberty* and *Free Gaza* sailed into Gaza Harbor from Cyprus carrying forty-four international supporters of the Palestinians. They were the first vessels to break the Israeli siege in forty-one years. The Free Gaza movement had the venture.

We passed within a mile of the Israeli natural gas platform servicing the Med Yavne deposit. It lies roughly 5 nautical miles from shore and 200 yards north of the Gaza Corridor. The Gaza Marine deposits are about 5 miles to the south and clearly within the Gaza Corridor. As we saw in Iraq, the Kuwaitis were accused of slant drilling into their neighbor's oil fields. There is speculation, though no available proof to date, that Israel is slant drilling into the Palestinian deposits.

October/November 2008: I joined other international observers traveling aboard three separate Gazan fishing boats. We went to document events and locations and to hopefully serve as deterrents against attacks by Israeli gunboats. On both days, we were harassed by machine gun and cannon fire, and explosive charges landing within a few feet of our boat. Several times each day, the largest of the three Israeli patrol boats came within 50 feet of our vessel as they raked the deck and cabin with a high pressure water cannon.

Any fish, loose equipment or crewmen caught in the torrent were at risk of being washed over the side. All the cabin windows had been previously smashed by such assaults and were now quickly boarded up when the patrol boats approached. An Italian observer with us had been wounded previously by flying glass, requiring a number of stitches in his back.

According to the crew, attacks of this sort occurred every day when a fishing boat approached or passed the 6-mile limit imposed by the Israelis. This pattern of attack began in 2000 after the natural gas discovery was made.

November 5, 2008: IDF forces killed 6 Palestinians while supposedly searching for a tunnel passing under the border. By continuing to enforce the siege, the Israelis never honored the conditions of the truce. But this incursion by the IDF was such a blatant violation; it effectively terminated even the semblance of a truce.

According to the Israeli Intelligence Heritage Center, one rocket had been fired from Gaza in September and 2 in October before the IDF incursion. Israeli spokesman Mark Regev conceded that Hamas had not fired these few rockets.

During the next 5 weeks, 237 rockets were fired into Israel.[20] The provoked increase in rocket fire was Israel's public justification for launching the long planned "Cast Lead" invasion despite offers by Hamas to renew the ceasefire.[21]

November 18, 2008: Israeli naval vessels attacked three Palestinian fishing boats located seven miles off the coast of Deir Al Balah, clearly within the limits permitted in the 1994 Gaza-Jericho Agreement. Fifteen Palestinian fishermen and three international observers were kidnapped and taken with the boats to Israel. The fishermen were held for a day and then released. The boats were eventually returned but damaged. The internationals were jailed in Israel for many days and then deported.

November 18, 2008: An Egyptian court ordered the government to stop shipping natural gas to Israel. Under a 2005 agreement, Egypt agreed to deliver 1.7 billion cubic meters of gas to Israel over a 15-year period. The gas began to flow in May 2008. A lawsuit followed, seeking to bar delivery, since the Parliament had not given its approval. The court supported the lawsuit and its findings are being appealed.[22] The potential cutoff of the gas from Egypt gave Israel even more incentive to take control of the Gaza Marine deposits and to deny any benefits to Palestinians whether Hamas or Fatah.

December 27, 2008: Israel begins bombing Gaza as phase 1 of operation "Cast Lead". The Gaza harbor was bombed during the hostilities, damaging a number of the fishing boats. More than 1400 Palestinians were killed, over 350 of them children.

January 18, 2009: Israel declared a ceasefire ending Operation "Cast Lead".

February 14, 2009: The Gaza coast becomes a no-go zone. On Saturday 14th February, 2009, 23 year-old Rafiq abu Reala was shot by Israeli naval forces while fishing in Gazan territorial waters, approximately two nautical miles out from the port of Gaza city. He was in a simple fishing vessel, not much larger than a rowing boat, with a small outboard engine, known locally as a 'hassaka'. Rafiq, his brother Rajab and another friend were following the course of a shoal of fish. A group of five more hassakas were out at the time, about a kilometer to the west of Rafiq's boat, further out to sea. An Israeli naval gunboat approached the area and began shooting at the other hassakas, which quickly changed course and headed east, back towards shore.

Suddenly Rafiq realized the gunboat was bearing down on their hassaka. As he recounted the events of that day, Rafiq likened the predatory nature of the naval vessel to that of a wolf. It circled their fishing boat and began shooting heavy ammunition in their direction. The three terrified fishermen threw themselves down flat in the bottom of their boat. The Israeli captain ordered them via megaphone to raise their nets and leave the area. At this point the gunboat was less than 20 meters from Rafiq's hassaka. The second time the gunboat came around, no attempt was made to communicate with the fishermen. Rafiq was desperately pulling in the nets with his back facing the gunboat. An M-16 assault rifle was fired hitting him twice with explosive 'dum-dum' bullets, which peppered his back with shrapnel from the bullets themselves.

The force of the shots threw him in the water, plunging him down about six or seven meters below the surface. Rajab asked their friend to control the boat while he rescued Rafiq. Being a strong swimmer, he dived in after Rafiq and pulled him out of the water into the hassaka. However, Rafiq was unconscious by this time. The outboard was being slowed down by the weight of the nets, so they headed towards another hassaka 300 meters away where they dumped the nets. The fishermen in this vessel had a mobile phone and made an emergency call. The stricken hassaka reached port at the same time as the ambulance arrived, and Rafiq was taken to Al-Shifa Hospital in Gaza city in a serious condition.

It would take Rafiq months to fully recover, yet he has a family to support. He had just married and his wife was expecting their first baby. After five years of working as a fisherman, he has experienced Israeli naval forces firing warning shots on many occasions; but this was the first time he has been directly targeted. However, Rajab survived being shot in the chest by the Israeli navy two and a half years ago. Eighteen Gaza fishermen have been killed by the Israeli navy between 2000 and 2011. [23]

Israel is attempting to create arbitrary 'no-go' zones in the sea – enforced solely by the gun. They might succeed if it weren't for the resilience of the fishermen. All this is akin to what is happening on land. The Israeli Occupation Force has declared an area of Palestinian land a kilometer in from the

Green Line a 'closed military zone', affecting an audacious land grab that threatens to swallow a vast swathe of rich agricultural land all the way along the eastern length of the Gaza strip." [24]

January 2009: Noble Energy announced the discovery of a vast deposit of natural gas some 50 miles off the Haifa shoreline. Named Tamar 1, it is estimated to hold 5 trillion cubic feet and be able to produce 50 per cent more than the daily capacity of the old Mari-B site. The stocks of Noble Energy and its partners, Delek Group and Avner Oil, have soared since the announcement.

March 30, 2009: Noble Energy announced the discovery of another major deposit at Dalit, located about 30 miles off shore from Israel. Production estimates have not been released, but the two discoveries are considered sufficient to cover Israel's energy needs for many years. [25]

These two huge gas deposits fall within an area called the Levant Basin that arcs from Egypt to Syria, extending north towards Cyprus. According to the U.S. Geological Survey the costal areas from Egypt north to Syria contain 122 trillion cubic feet of natural gas and 1.7 billion barrels of recoverable oil. Already, maritime boundaries have been disputed, with Lebanon claiming Israeli incursions into their territorial waters. They have requested the United Nations survey and clarify their borders, but have been rebuffed. The UN spokesman stated that Resolution 1701 "does not include the demarcation of maritime borders. National conflicts and maritime conflicts are two separate things." Israel's minister of national infrastructures, Uzi Landau, has stated that they would "not hesitate to use force" to protect the gas fields. [26]

2011/2012: Turkey has expressed concern over a joint Israeli-Greek Cypriot venture to explore for natural gas in Greek Cypriot waters. Thus far the Turks have limited their response to shadowing research vessels with planes and boats, but the potential for more significant confrontations exists. Turkish Prime Minister Erdogan has stated: "Turkey will not allow Israel to exploit 'one-sided,' the natural gas deposits in the eastern Mediterranean." [27]

The effort of the Palestinians to gain even limited recognition in the United Nations raises the prospects of another area of conflict. Despite the discovery of the huge Tamar-1 deposit, it is not expected to begin delivery until 2014 at the earliest. In the interest of finding a more quickly developed resource, Israel has demanded permission from the gas company Noble Energy to start developing the Gaza Marine deposits that were discovered in 1999 within Gazan waters.

However, if the Palestinians are granted even limited recognition by the UN, they would surely assert a more credible legal claim to the natural gas deposits off their shore. In such an event, energy-poor Turkey may well support the Palestinians' claim to the deposits more actively than in the past.

March, 2009 – Present: Attacks by Israeli gunboats on the Gazan fishermen continued unabated. Dozens of Gazan fishermen have been injured, some killed, or abducted to Israel. Many continue to have their boats confiscated. Although Israel supposedly allows fishing within 3 nautical miles of shore, their war ships attack fishing boats at random and without provocation, sometimes only a few hundred meters off shore.

The stated Israeli justification is that weapons might be smuggled ashore. It is the same canard used against the Flotillas attempting to bring goods and passengers to Gaza. In fact, the two main purposes for Israel's illegal blockade are: 1- To further tighten the economic noose around Gaza by further restricting the inflow of essential goods and the outflow of exports that could help revitalize a failed economy; and 2- To deny the Palestinians access to natural gas deposits that lie under their waters and that would bring them income and energy independence.

215

It remains one more Israeli crime where the U.S. Government is pointedly silent.

Darlene Wallach is inspecting the damage on a Gaza fishing boat, attacked by the Israeli navy while trying to fish in Gaza waters.

216

Chapter 12: Epilogue

Greta

We've all caught Gaza fever: every one of us who works to send boats to Gaza. From August 2006, when a handful of us started the Free Gaza movement, everyone who has joined us has been stricken with a bad case of the disease. It is chronic. It sometimes causes afflicted patients to insist that if just one more voyage can be planned to this small slice of the Mediterranean, we'll all be in remission. There is no real cure in sight... yet.

Gaza Fever has now attacked thousands of us who feel a passionate sense of justice for the Palestinians. The disease began shortly after Israel invaded Lebanon in 2006, as a group of us were in despair that the Palestinians, once again, were the forgotten symptom of Israel's grand designs. As the world watched the defeat of Israel by a small band of guerrilla fighters in Lebanon, Israel decided it would take its wrath out on the Palestinians, specifically the Palestinians of Gaza. Our small idea of sailing boats to Gaza to break Israel's illegal siege there has grown. We, who have traveled by boat to Gaza, come back changed, blisters of outrage forever marking us. Those who have supported us through donations, letters and picketing in front of Israeli Embassies, demanding Israel stop its war crimes against a civilian population, are also changed, as they watched our small boats sail into Gaza five times, cheering us on our way.

Will there be a cure? Only if their fishermen can fish without being shot and murdered; only if their farmers can harvest their crops without Israeli military vehicles burning down their wheat; only if Gaza has the same rights as every country on the Mediterranean... the right to free and open trade with the rest of the world. Then and only then will our severe case of Gaza Fever be cured.

OJ is being welcomed to Gaza by thousands. She elected to stay and work in Gaza.

Because of this first success at breaking Israel's illegal siege on 1.5 million people, donors stepped up and purchased a yacht named *Dignity*, which made four successful voyages to Gaza from October through December 2008. On its fifth voyage, as Israel was committing massacres on the people of Gaza in an attack called Operation Cast Lead, an Israeli warship deliberately rammed the Dignity three times while she was still in international waters, severely damaging the vessel and endangering the lives of the sixteen civilians onboard. Fortunately she was able to make it to safety in Sidon, Lebanon, without sinking.

We watched as Israel, in January 2009, deliberately bombed 1.5 million Palestinians into abject poverty, a man-made catastrophe bordering on genocide.

Undeterred, we bought a fourth vessel, the *Spirit of Humanity (Arion)* that was nearly capsized by the Israeli Navy as we sailed in emergency care workers and medical supplies in

January 2009. The boat was forced to turn back in rough waters.

On June 30, 2009 while making another attempt to reach Gaza, the *Spirit of Humanity* was boarded and hijacked by the Israeli Navy. All twenty-one unarmed civilian passengers were imprisoned in Israel. Two of the passengers who hold Israeli citizenship were released. After about a week, the remaining nineteen *Spirit* passengers were deported to their various host countries.

We organized for almost a year, knowing that sending in only one or two boats would not make a difference to the Palestinians and Israel's draconian siege on them. We determined that the only way for the world to wake up to the collective punishment inflicted on a civilian population was to increase the size of the boats and the number of people going. May 31, 2010, while clearly in international waters sixty-five miles off the coast of Israel, a small fleet of six vessels known as the Freedom Flotilla was lethally attacked and illegally boarded by Israeli commandoes. Eight Turkish nationals and one American were killed aboard the *Mavi Marmara,* the largest ship in the flotilla. Another Turkish passenger has been in a terminal coma since the attack with no hope of ever surviving. On all other ships, the passengers were beaten, tear gassed, some with bones were thrown on the ground and handcuffed.

This act of Israeli aggression provoked worldwide condemnation and raised global awareness about the ongoing illegal siege of Gaza. Five days later, the Israeli Navy seized the *MV Rachel Corrie,* a cargo ship carrying reconstruction and education supplies for the people of Gaza. Again, the unarmed passengers were forced to the ground, handcuffed, and held on deck in the blazing sun guarded by dogs and heavily armed Israeli commandoes.

We were still not going to be stopped and spent another year organizing Freedom Flotilla 2, a larger fleet with more than 32 countries involved. We were going to sail on the anniversary of the murders or our passengers in May 2010. However, Israel and the US outsourced the occupation to Greece where most of the boats were moored, and we were stopped before we could pull out of port. However, we made our point; that a band of international activists could and did drive major governments into having nervous breakdowns over our attempts to sail to the illegally blockaded port of Gaza.

As we write this book in the spring of 2012, another voyage of two small boats with passengers from Canada, Belgium, Denmark, Palestine, Israel, Egypt, the U.S., and Ireland was brutally stopped in November 2011. The boats were hijacked in international waters by the Israeli navy while sailing to Gaza, then hauled into Israel where none of us wanted to go, and our passengers rounded up and sent to prison, then deported. The reason? Israeli authorities say we entered Israel illegally. The chutzpah that it takes to come up with that excuse is mindboggling.

And a new initiative, **Gaza's Ark**, is being organized by the Canadian Boat to Gaza, along with several of our coalition partners. We are pushing the envelope and turning the voyages around; sailing a boat from Gaza into international waters and on to Europe, delivering products from the people of Gaza to markets throughout Europe: a small step for Gaza and a giant step for humankind.

Nothing Israel will do is going to stop our voyages. We will continue to sail. As long as Gaza is blockaded, we will return. Unfortunately, the strangulation of the Palestinians in Gaza continues; therefore, the work of the Free Gaza movement and now many other partners, is only beginning.

About the Authors

Gamaal Al-Attar, (Gaza) Gamaal is a Palestinian urban designer. He was born in Sudan in 1984, and was first educated in Egypt before moving to Gaza, Palestine in 1994 with his family. He continued his education in UNRWA (United Nation Relief and Works Agency) schools and took his Bachelor's degree in Architectural Engineering at the Islamic University of Gaza in 2008. He will finish his master's degree in urban design and city development at the University of Stavanger, Norway in 2013.

Gamaal has been active in Scouting since 1998 and it was the main activity for him throughout school and his professional life. Gamaal was a voluntary activist with the first End the Blockade Campaign in Gaza and was there to meet the first two boats.

Vittorio Arrigoni, (Italy) Vik had a wide experience in international charity work in the battle for human rights in Eastern Europe and Africa. In 2003, he made his first visit to Palestine, initially in a work camp managed by International Palestinian Youth League in Eastern Jerusalem and later in Nablus in the Balata refugee camp. In 2006, he attempted to return to Palestine, but was denied entry.

Held in Israeli detention for a week while appealing the decision, he was then expelled from the country. In August 2006, at the request of the European Union, Vittorio attended the first free elections in the Democratic Republic of the Congo as an international observer. He was on the *Free Gaza* during the maiden voyage and then stayed in Gaza to do human rights work. After being abducted and deported in Gaza waters by the Israeli Navy in November 2008, he returned to Gaza on *The Dignity,* another FG boat a month later. He was there during the winter of 2008-2009, and his

221

book, Gaza: Stay Human (Kube Publishing, 2010), is his eyewitness testimony of the attack. Vittorio managed one of the most popular blogs in Italy at:

On April 14, 2011, Vik was murdered in his beloved Gaza by a little-known faction there. His tragic death has devastated the activist and Palestinian community who knew and loved him for his joy of life. The second Freedom Flotilla was named STAY HUMAN in his honor. http://www.guerrillaradio.iobloggo.com.

Greta Berlin, (US, France) Greta is one of the five co-founders of the Free Gaza movement. Greta has worked for justice for the Palestinians since the early 1960s. She is the mother of two Palestinian-American children whose father was born and raised in Safad, Palestine and was forced to flee from there in 1948. She has been an outspoken advocate for the rights of Palestinians, and has spoken and written extensively on the issue.

Greta has been in the West Bank three times since 2003 working with the International Solidarity Movement (ISM) in the occupied towns of Bil'in, Jenin or Ramallah or working in the media office. She was wounded in the leg by an Israeli rubber-coated steel bullet in July 2003 while protesting Israel's apartheid wall. She was on the first boat into Gaza and has either organized or been in charge of the land and media team for most of the other voyages of the Free Gaza movement. When not working for the rights of Palestinians, Greta teaches engineers and scientists how to design and deliver presentations.

Lauren Booth, (UK) A broadcaster and journalist, Lauren first traveled to the West Bank in 2005, and returned in 2007 and 2009. While living in Gaza, she witnessed the daily humiliations suffered by the Palestinian people under occupation. During the first Free Gaza mission, Lauren was aboard one of the ships to break Israel's sea blockade of the Palestinian coast—an experience she describes as the greatest moment of her life. She presents the groundbreaking program "Remember Palestine" on Press TV, working closely with a variety of groups, committed to ending Israel's illegal occupation and the siege of Gaza.

Renee Bowyer, (UK, Australia) Renee Bowyer, also known as Eliza Ernshire (a pseudonym she used while living and working in the West Bank between 2005 and 2007) is an Australian activist who has been involved with the Free Gaza movement since its beginning as is one of the five Co-Founders.

From an early age, she was interested in working with refugee communities, first travelling to the Northwest Frontier of Pakistan during the American led invasion of Afghanistan to work with the Afghan refugee communities there. In 2005, she chose to focus her time and efforts on the Palestinian struggle and spent years living in the Middle East; first in the refugee camps of Jordan, then the Occupied Territories of Palestine and finally in Lebanon.

She met her husband and father of her two small children, Fathi Jaouadi, on the first voyage to Gaza and since then, both Renee and Fathi have remained very active in the Free Gaza movement. These two children were the first Free Gaza babies.

Bill Dienst, M.D. (US) Bill is a family and emergency room physician from the Okanogan Valley in rural Washington in the Pacific Northwest of the United States. In 1985, after an intensive summer course in Arabic, Bill took an extra year of medical school and spent six months in Egypt, the West Bank and Gaza volunteering with various Palestinian health care organizations, initially with the Palestine Red Crescent Society, which was headquartered in Egypt. He has been to Palestine six times on trips sponsored by the Gaza Community Mental Health Programme, by Washington Physicians for Social

Responsibility, and with the Palestine Medical Relief Society. He was on the maiden voyage of the Free Gaza movement

Mona El Farra, M.D. (Gaza, Palestine) Dr. Mona is a Palestinian from Gaza who wears many hats. She is a physician by trade and a human and women's rights activist by practice. She is currently the chair of Gaza Red Crescent, Heath Care Committee but has also worked with Al Awda Hospital in Jabalya refugee camp and Union of Health Workers Committee. She is also the projects director in Gaza for the Middle East Children's Alliance (MECA).

Musheir El Farra, (UK, Gaza) Musheir is a political and human rights activist. He is a consultant Civil and Structural Engineer by profession. He was born in 1961 in the town of Khan Younis at the southern part of the Gaza Strip.

Musheir is the Chair of Sheffield Palestine Solidarity Campaign in England and was a member of the Executive committee of the National Palestine Solidarity in Britain for six years. For 16 years, Musheir has coordinated, on behalf of Sheffield PSC, supporting three children's centres in Jabalya and Nuseirat refugee camps, and Khan Younis town.

He frequently publishes articles in different Arabic newspapers on social and political issues. Musheir is an active public speaker in Britain for the rights of the Palestinian people. He also wrote the scripts, coordinated and narrated three films on Palestine. Currently he is writing a book on Operation Cast Lead, the Israeli massacres in the Gaza Strip in 2008/2009.

Independent MP Jamal El-Khoudary, Ph.D. (Gaza) A Palestinian Legislative Council member, The Head of the Popular Committee Against Siege on Gaza, Ex-minister of Telecommunications and Information Technology, one of the main contacts in Gaza who helped organize the welcome.

Petros Giotis, (Greece) Petros Giotis was born in 1956 in Filippiada, a small town of Epirus, Greece. After high school in Filippiada, he went to Salonika and completed a chemical engineering degree at Polytechnic University. Petros has worked as a journalist since his early university years; he eventually became a professional journalist. Today, he is the chief editor for the Greek newspaper KONTRA. For many years he has been a pro-Palestinian author and activist.

Riad Hamad, (Lebanon and USA) Riad was a longtime peace activist and educator in Austin, Texas. A lifelong scholar, Riad received the first of many degrees from the University of Texas, Austin and was pursuing a Ph.D. in Educational Technology. Riad touched many lives as an educator and friend. He was a computer technology instructor at Clint Small Middle School. He was a selfless individual who focused on helping students realize their potential. He was also a champion of human rights and worked tirelessly for peace and justice. He founded the Palestine Children's Welfare Fund to aid Palestinian children, women, and families in need.

He died tragically on April 14, 2008 under suspicious circumstances. Although his death was ruled a suicide, constant harassment by the U.S. government is believed to be the cause.

Jeff Halper, Ph.D. (Israel) Jeff is an Israeli professor of anthropology and coordinator of the Israeli Committee Against House Demolitions (ICAHD), a nonviolent Israeli peace and human rights organization that resists the Israeli occupation. In 2006, the American Friends Service Committee nominated Jeff to receive the 2006 Nobel Peace Prize with Palestinian intellectual and activist Ghassan Andoni.

Mary Hughes Thompson, (US, UK) Mary is a retired TV documentarian and a Co-Founder of the Free Gaza movement.

Before helping break the siege of Gaza on board the *Free Gaza,* she visited the West Bank six times during the current intifada. In 2002 she was beaten and robbed by American-Jewish youths from the illegal settlement of Itamar near Nablus. Mary has returned to the occupied West Bank to work with the ISM and has also worked several times in Cyprus as part of the Free Gaza land team, most recently during the Freedom Flotilla voyage.

She is also a licensed pilot. A long time nonviolent activist for Palestine, she was also a participant in the Gaza Freedom March in Cairo.

Paul Larudee, Ph.D. (US) Paul, a Co-Founder of the Free Gaza movement, is a San Francisco Bay Area activist on the issue of justice in the region known as Palestine, which includes Israel, the West Bank, the Gaza Strip, and Jerusalem. He was born to an Iranian Presbyterian minister and his American missionary spouse in 1946. He grew up in the American Midwest and has been to the occupied West Bank several times as a member of the ISM. He is currently a Co-Founder of the Free Palestine Movement.

Sharyn Lock, (Australia, UK) Sharyn is originally from Australia but now lives in the United Kingdom. A veteran ISM activist in the West Bank, she was badly wounded in an Israeli attack there while working with the ISM in the occupied West Bank. She is one of the co-founders of Free Gaza. After making the initial FG trip, she returned on the *Dignity* and was on the ground with other FG/ISM activists who directly witnessed the twenty-two-day Israeli assault on Gaza in December 2008-January 2009 called Operation Cast Lead.

Her book, *Gaza Beneath the Bombs* (2010, Pluto Press, with Sarah Irving), is her eyewitness account of the attacks. For many years, she fit community work around environmental and human rights campaigning. Her time spent in Palestine led her to acquire basic medical skills, and she is currently a student midwife in the United Kingdom.

Aki Nawaz, (UK, Pakistan) Aki Nawaz is a producer/musician and part of the band Fun-Da-Mental. He is best known for his controversial lyrics. Aki grew up in Bradford, England. His parents were Pakistani immigrants who arrived in England in 1964. He was the drummer in Southern Death Cult, which became the Cult. After various bands, Aki moved to London, set up a management company and signed artists to major record labels. Two years later, he formed Nation Records as a label primarily focused on creating fusions between different musical forms from all over the world for a more youth-oriented audience.

Changing musical genres, Nawaz went on to found the Islamic rap group, Fun-Da-Mental. In 1991, he set up Nation Records. He was the group's leader, as the most visible and outspoken member politically and culturally, and is a pro-active activist.

Aki has collaborated with many traditional musicians, both in the studio and live, including Huun Huur Tu, Rizwan Muazzam Qawwal, Mighty Zulu Nation (a South African hip-hop group), and many others.

Vangelis Pissias, Ph.D. (Greece) Vangelis is a professor of water engineering at the Technical University of Athens. He is the person who bought and outfitted the two fishing boats that took us to Gaza. He has been a long-time activist for Palestine and was part of the Greek underground during the time of the Generals in Greece (1967-1974).

Mazin Qumsiyeh, Ph.D. (US, Palestine) Professor Mazin Qumsiyeh teaches and does research at Bethlehem and Birzeit Universities in occupied Palestine. He serves as chairman of the board of the Palestinian Center for Rapprochement

Between People and is the coordinator of the Popular Committee Against the Wall and Settlements in Beit Sahour. He is author of: <u>Sharing the Land of Canaan</u>: *Human Rights and the Israeli/Palestinian Struggle* and <u>Popular Resistance in Palestine</u>: *A History of Hope and Empowerment.*

Yvonne Ridley, (UK) Yvonne is from County Durham in the United Kingdom and is a TV presenter, author and activist. She first came to prominence when arrested and held for ten days by the Taliban in Afghanistan following the 9/11 atrocity. She was released on humanitarian grounds. A founding member of Stop the Wall and the Respect Party, she had been trying to enter Gaza for many years to show solidarity with the people trapped there. After arriving on the initial FG voyage, she has returned to Gaza as part of the Viva Palestina! land convoy.

David K. Schermerhorn, (US) David is a commercial film producer and is eighty-one years young. He was part of the crew of the *Free Gaza* on its voyage to Gaza in August 2008. He is an explorer, adventurer and has traveled around the world on boats. He has been part of the crew on almost every voyage and was on the *Challenger 1* in May 2010 when Israel attacked the flotilla.

Hillary Smith, (UK) Hillary lives in Sheffield, England, and has long been an advocate in Palestinian solidarity work there. She has been involved in grassroots organizing, particularly in the initial grant and fund-raising efforts that made the Free Gaza movement possible. She continues to do media support work on behalf of Free Gaza.

Michael Shaik, (Australia) Michael became involved in the Palestinian struggle for independence when, in 2003, he was the Media Coordinator in Beit Sahour for the ISM. Following his deportation from Israel-Palestine, he has worked to raise awareness of the Palestinians' struggle among the Australian public and first thought of using ships to break the blockade of the Gaza Strip following Israel's "disengagement" in 2005. He worked as the Public Advocate for Australians for Palestine from 2007 to 2010, is a contributor to two books on the role of non-violent direct action in the struggle for Palestinian independence and has commented on Israeli-Palestinian affairs for The Australian, The Age, The Canberra Times, ABC Radio National, and SBS television and radio.

Ren Tawil, (US) Ren was born in his mother's hometown, San Francisco, California (USA) in 1953. His father Afif George Tawil was born and raised in Jerusalem, Palestine, and was visiting the United States in May 1948. As a result he could not freely return to the land of his birth and became a 'displaced person'. Ren first became aware of the politics surrounding the 'Palestinian Problem' after the June War of 1967 as an 8th grader, and has maintained an interest ever since. He was on the first voyage to Gaza in August, 2008.

Donna Wallach, (US) Donna is an anti-Zionist activist working for social and environmental justice. She lives in San Jose, California (USA), and is of Eastern European-Jewish descent. She lived in occupied Palestine in the Tel Aviv area from 1981 to 1997 and experienced firsthand the impact of the brutal Israeli occupation on Palestinians living inside Israel, as well as the Palestinians in the occupied West Bank and Gaza.

She was in Ramallah during the 2002 siege and spent a week in the Gaza Strip at that time. She shares the grief and outrage of the boat crew that all historic Palestine is still occupied by the apartheid state of Israel. After arriving on the first Free Gaza movement boats, she stayed as a long-term volunteer until December 2008

Col. Ann Wright, (US) Ann is a twenty-nine-year veteran of the U.S. Army and U.S. Army Reserves who retired as a colonel. She served sixteen years in the U.S. Diplomatic Corps in U.S. Embassies in Nicaragua, Grenada, Somalia, Uzbekistan, Kyrgyzstan, Sierra Leone, Micronesia, Afghanistan, and Mongolia. She was deputy ambassador in the last four embassies where she served.

Acknowledgements

Thank you to the thousands of you who donated to us and believed in us. From the moment we began this journey, people stepped up to help; the dozens of people around the world who stepped up to raise money for us by going out in the community and talking about a project none of us were sure was really going to happen; the 10-member land team in Cyprus who didn't get to go and were there covering our backs or working in their countries to send out media messages; and those of you who called the Israeli Embassies around the world when our communication systems were cut off and demanded that Israel turn them back on. They include Ramzi Kysia, Osama Qashoo, Scott Kennedy, Uri Davis, Angela Godfrey-Goldstein, David Halpin, M.D., Sue Halpin, Steve Greaves, Lynn Levey, and Jonny Loveboat.

From the Greek side, we would like to thank Marcos Garas, Maria Dimitriadi, Tania Dimitriadi, Mihalis Tiktopoulos, Spiros Giotis and Giannis Thanos. From Cyprus, we'd like to thank Nora Shawwa and Elli Mozora, plus the wonderful journalists who followed our adventure, wrote about us and didn't think we were crazy.

Thank you to Anis Hamadah, who designed and ran our website for us during that first trip, wrote songs for us and created wonderful pieces of artwork as well.

We would also like to thank the proofreaders of this book: Jane Jewell, Gerri Haynes, Rod Such, Pam Olson, Rick Gillespie, and Roxanne Summers.

And thank you, Darlene Wallach, for adding an index.

End Notes

Foreword

1. Col. Ann Wright letter of resignation
   http://www.govexec.com/defense/2003/03/mary-a-wrights-resignation-letter/13704

Chapter 1: You Will Never Make it

1. Palestinians' 'Return Ship' Hit by Blast: Bombing in Cyprus Halts Protest Voyage; PLO Blames Israel, 2/88
   http://articles.latimes.com/1988-02-16/news/mn-42970_1_protest-voyage

Chapter 2: In Memory of Riad Hamad

1. A View - Middle East, Obituary-Riad Hamad, 05/08
   http://www.globalresearch.ca/index.php?context=va&aid=8741
2. KLBJ Radio, Austin Local News, 04/17/08
   http://www.590klbj.com/News/Story.aspx?ID=89235
3. C.L. Cook, Pacific Free Press, Riad Hamad, A Death in Austin, 04/19/08
   http://pacificfreepress.com/content/view/2509/1/
4. The Austin Chronicle, The Uneasy Death of Riad Hamad, 05/09/08
   http://www.austinchronicle.com/news/2008-05-09/621848/

Chapter 3: Athenian Spooks

1. Barak Ravid, "Israel fears European ship may sail to Gaza to 'break siege,'" *Haaretz*, July 28, 2008 http://www.haaretz.com/print-edition/news/israel-fears-european-ship-may-sail-to-gaza-to-break-siege-1.250634

Chapter 8: We Are Coming, We Have Arrived

1. Musheir El Farra, Gaza, When The Sky Rained White Fire, Israeli War Crimes In The Gaza Strip
2. Reprinted from, Sharyn Lock, Gaza Beneath the Bombs, (London: Pluto Press, 2010), 12-14
3. Vittorio Arrigoni, Guerilla Radio, 08/25/08, translated by Sharyn Lock

Chapter 9: Getting to Know Gaza

1. Reference notes regarding internment camp and concentration camp:
   - Internment Camp (n) A camp where prisoners of war and hostile aliens are kept during a war.
   - Concentration Camp (n A camp, where civilians or political prisoners, and sometimes prisoners of war are detained and confined, typically under harsh conditions or a place or situation characterized by extremely harsh conditions.
   - Civilian internee is a special status of a prisoner under the Fourth Geneva Convention. Civilian internees are civilians who are detained by a party to a war for security reasons.
   - The Fourth Geneva Convention relates to the protection of civilians during times of war. It specifies that those "in the hands" of an enemy and under any military

occupation by a foreign power may not be punished for an offense he or she has not personally committed. Reprisals against protected persons and their property are prohibited.
http://www.newworldencyclopedia.org/entry/concentration_camp
http://www.allwords.com/word-internment+camp.html

Chapter 11: Stealing Gaza's Gas, the Real Reason for the Illegal Blockade on Gaza

1. Andrew Muncie's Video. 10/08
   http://www.youtube.com/watch?v=PAUzugKX1AE
2. Gaza-Jericho Agreement, 05/04/99, Bloomberg.com
3. UN Convention on the Law of the Sea Part V, Article 55
4. Peter Eyre interview on Energy World
5. Matthew Carr, The Guardian, Palestinians missing out on a £2bn energy fortune
   http://www.theweek.co.uk/politics/24477/palestinians-missing-out-%C2%A32bn-energy-fortune#ixzz1uURCdR6
6. Sasha Polakow-Suransky, Who Killed Camp David?
   09/19/04, http://prospect.org/article/who-killed-camp-david
7. Julian Borgor, Anger at Peace Talk Meddling, 07/13/00,
   http://www.guardian.co.uk/world/2000/jul/13/israel2
8. Peter Eyre interview on Energy World, 2009
   http://www.presstv.ir/Programs/player/?id=84338
9. Arthur Neslin, Gaza: A Gas for Tony Blair? 07/26/07,
   http://www.guardian.co.uk/commentisfree/2007/jul/26/gazaagasforblair
10. Extra, Sharon Elected, 02/07/01
    http://www.pbs.org/newshour/extra/features/jan-june01/israel_election.htmll
11. Interviews with Gaza fishermen, David Schermerhorn
12. Wikipedia Directional Drilling
    http://en.wikipedia.org/wiki/Directional_drilling
13. United Nations Mission Report of Catherine Bertini
    http://domino.un.org/bertini_rpt.htm

14. Pepijn Koster, 07/01/07
    http://www.myfavouriteplaces.org/wl/pivot/entry.php?id=52
15. www.uruknet.info ISM 11/05/08
16. Israeli intelligence blackmails Gaza fishermen, 04/09/09
    http://www.uruknet.de/?p=53272
17. Ian Black, The Guardian, Six months of secret planning, then
    Israel moves against Hamas, 12/29/08
18. Michel Chossudovsky, War and Natural Gas, The Israeli
    Invasion and Gaza's Offshore Gas Fields, Global Research,
    01/08/09
    http://globalresearch.ca/index.php?context=va&aid=11680
19. Ibid.
20. Isabel Kershner, Gaza Rocket Fire Intensifies, New York Times
    12/25/08
21. Operation Cast Lead, Global Security.org
    http://www.globalsecurity.org/military/world/war/operation
    -cast-lead.htm
22. Ibid.
23. http://www.youtube.com/watch?v=koWUY84c02M
24. Expanding illegal no-go zones leaves 100s homeless, Gaza,
    01/30/09
    http://ingaza.wordpress.com/2009/01/30/expanding-illegal-
    no-go-zones-leaves-100s-homeless/
25. Noble Energy Announces Second Natural Gas Discovery
    Offshore Israel at Dalit, 03/30/09
    http://investors.nobleenergyinc.com/releasedetail.cfm?releas
    eid=373732
26. Ibrahim Saif, Sami Atallah, Ali Berro, Walid Khadouri, Gas in the
    Levant Basin: Another Source of Regional Conflict? 10/20/11
    http://carnegieendowment.org/2011/10/20/gas-in-lebanon-
    facts-challenges-and-future-prospects/8gja
27. Turkish Minister threatens Cyprus about oil in the Mediterranean,
    Cyprus Expat, 04/09/11
    http://www.cyprusexpat.co.uk/blog/read/id:183/

Appendix A: Passenger List for *Free Gaza* and *Liberty*

1. Giorgos Klontzas, 38 (Greece), Captain, *Liberty*
2. John Klusmire, 60 (USA), Captain, *Free Gaza*
3. Huwaida Arraf, LLD, 32 (USA and Palestine) Attorney and professor, Co-Founder, International Solidarity Movement (ISM), *Liberty*
4. Vittorio Arrigoni, 33 (Italy) Journalist for Guerilla Radio http://guerrillaradio.iobloggo.com Murdered in Gaza on April 15, 2011, *Free Gaza*
5. Greta Berlin, 67, (USA, France) Business owner, Co-Founder, Free Gaza, *Free Gaza*
6. Lauren Booth, 41 (UK) Journalist for Press TV and London Sunday Times, *Free Gaza*
7. Renee Bowyer, 32 (Australia) Music teacher, Co-Founder, Free Gaza, *Liberty*
8. Nikolas Bolos (Nikos), 51 (Greece) Chemist and crew member, *Liberty*
9. Ayash Darraji (Algeria) Al Jazeera journalist, *Free Gaza*
10. Maria Del Mar 53 (Spain) Criminal attorney, *Free Gaza*
11. Bill Dienst, M.D., 49 (USA) Family and Emergency room physician, *Liberty*
12. Musheir El Farra, 47 (Gaza/UK) Civil and Structural engineer, *Free Gaza*
13. Giorgos K (Greece) delegate; Greek Association for Solidarity with the Palestinian People INTIFADA, *Free Gaza*
14. Petros Giotis, 52 (Greece) Journalist and author, *Liberty*
15. Christos Giouanopoulos (Greece) Cinematographer and crew member, *Free Gaza*
16. Derek Graham, 42 (Ireland/Cyprus) Electrician and first mate, *Free Gaza*

17. Jeff Halper, Ph.D., 62 (Israel), Professor of Anthropology Head of Israeli Committee Against House Demolitions, *Free Gaza*
18. Fathi Jaouadi, 36 (Tunisia) Working on MA in Documentary Film-making at Brunel University in London, *Free Gaza*
19. Hayyan Jubeh, (Jerusalem, Palestine) Ramattan journalist, *Free Gaza*
20. Yiannis Karipidis, 51 (Greece) Cinematographer, *Liberty*
21. The Hon. Anastasios Kourakis (Tasos), M.D., MP (representing Thessaloniki, Greece), *Liberty*
22. Paul Larudee, Ph.D. 62 (USA) Piano tuner, Co-Founder, Free Gaza, *Liberty*
23. Edith Lutz, Ph.D., 59 (Germany) Nurse and teacher, *Liberty*
24. Jenny Linnell (O.J.), 34 (UK) Scuba diver, boat expert and crew member, *Liberty*
25. Sharyn Lock (Bella), 34 (Australia) Midwife, Co-Founder, Free Gaza, *Free Gaza*
26. Theresa McDermott, 41 (Scotland) Postal logistics worker, *Liberty*
27. Sister Anne Montgomery, 81 (USA), Catholic nun of religious Order of Sacred Heart, *Liberty*
28. Andrew Muncie, 34 (Scotland) Poker player with a philosophy degree, *Liberty*
29. Haq Nawaz Qureishi, Aki Nawaz, 26 (Pakistan/UK) Muscian and record label owner, *Liberty*
30. Thomas H. Nelson, LLD, 59 (USA) Attorney and Co-Founder of Americans United for Palestinian Human Rights, *Free Gaza*
31. Ken O'Keefe, 39 (Ireland) Owner of dive shop, scuba diver and crew member, *Free Gaza*
32. Panagiotis Politis (Takis), Ph.D., 48 (Greece) professor at the University of Thessalia, Greece, *Liberty*
33. Peter Philips, 28 (USA) IT specialist, *Free Gaza*

34. Vangelis Pissias, Ph.D. 61 (Greece) Professor of water engineering, boat buyer, *Liberty*
35. Adam Qvist, 22 (Denmark) Essayist, co-author of the novel "City Might Fall", *Liberty*
36. Yvonne Ridley (UK) Press TV journalist, author, captured by Taliban in 2002, *Liberty*
37. David K. Schermerhorn, 79 (USA) Film producer and crew member, *Free Gaza*
38. Courtney Sheetz, 25 (USA) Student and videographer, *Free Gaza*
39. Kathy Sheetz, 61 (USA) Nurse and grassroots organizer in Haiti, *Free Gaza*
40. Ren (Lawrence) Afif Tawil (USA) Activist and writer, *Free Gaza*
41. Mary Hughes Thompson, 71 Canada) TV writer, Co-Founder, Free Gaza, *Free Gaza*
42. Donna Wallach, 57 (Israel/USA) Grassroots organizer in Israel and U.S., *Free Gaza*
43. Darlene Wallach, 57 (USA) IT specialist, *Liberty*
44. Kathleen O'Connor Wang, 64 (USA) Real estate owner and grandmother, *Free Gaza*

Appendix B: <u>Gaza Chronology Leading up to Operation Cast Lead Attacks by Israel</u>

19th June: Ceasefire agreement between Israel and the Hamas government comes into force for six months. Israel insisted on a verbal agreement. It stated: cessation of all military hostilities on both sides, opening of Gaza's borders after seventy-two hours for 30 percent more trade and unrestricted trade after ten days. Egypt supports the extension of the agreement to the West Bank. (Source: International Crisis Group: Ending the War in Gaza. Middle East Briefing No. 26, 5.1.2009, 3)

19th June: Israeli warships fire four rockets at Palestinian fishermen in Palestinian waters. On the same day aircraft circling over Gaza City break the sound barrier near the ground and trigger a panic among the people. In the area of Khan Younis, Israeli patrols shoot over the border fence at farmers who work on their fields on the other side of the border. (Source: Ma'an, 26.06.2008). This scenario is repeated almost daily.

24th June: Two young officials of Jihad are murdered in their homes in Nablus by units of the IOF (Israeli Occupation [Defense] Force). On the same day, al-Quds Brigades fire three rockets at Sderot in retaliation. (Source: Ma'an 24.06.2008) The Israeli side uses the action of Jihad as an excuse to close the border crossings again.

26th June: The al-Aqsa Brigades fire a rocket on Sderot after many Fatah members have been arrested in raids by the Israeli army. With this, the al-Aqsa Brigades want to force the extension of the cease fire to the West Bank. The spokesman of the Hamas government in Gaza warns the al-Aqsa Brigades that their actions would prevent the lifting of the blockade and favor instead the narrower interests of an organizational and political nature.

29th June: A delegation of farmers complains to the Hamas Ministry of Agriculture that, because of the Israeli bombardment, they can no longer cultivate their fields along the border fence.

4th August: During a meeting of the Israeli labor party, the minister of defense, Ehud Barak, threatens a ground invasion into the Gaza strip, despite Hamas' adherence to the cease fire.

8th August: The director of the secret service Shin Bet, Yuval Diskin, thinks that a cease fire would reduce the pressure on Hamas to release Shalit. He calls on the army to prepare for a major military offensive. (Source: Ma'an 8.8.2008) These statements reinforce the impression among Palestinians that, as far as the Israeli military leadership is concerned, the purpose of the ceasefire is to gain time in order to prepare an offensive.

23rd August: Free Gaza's first two boats arrive in Gaza with no interference from Israel. Forty-four passengers joyously welcomed by 40,000 people on the shoreline.

9th September: The Israeli Navy sinks a fishing boat http://www.btselem.org/english/testimonies/20080910_israeli_navy_boat_charges_into_a_fishing_boat_witness_al_hasi.asp, after fishing boats were shot at and rammed several times.

25th October: The second Free Gaza boat arrives in Gaza on our new boat, the *Dignity*, carrying Mairead Maguire, Nobel Peace Laureate and others. Again, we were not stopped

4th November: Israeli troops enter into Khan Younis. Deliberately targeted projectiles kill six Hamas members and injure several people, including one woman. In the Deir al-Balah refugee camp, several rockets are fired at residential areas. Near Wadi Salqa, two houses of the Hawaidi family are destroyed and seven family members, three of them women, are kidnapped and taken to Israel. The same day Israeli border guards prevent French consular officials, who want to get a picture of the situation, from entering the Gaza strip. (Some background information: the dubious tunneler, Abu Dawabah, is arrested and claims, during interrogation, that both Hamas and al-Aqsa brigades had offered him money for kidnapping an Israeli soldier. (Source: Ma'an 3.11.2008) One day later, the Hamas Ministry of Internal Affairs issues a denial. (See also International Crisis Group: Ending the War in Gaza. Middle East Briefing No. 26, 5.1.2009, p.5)

5th November: Residential areas in the north of the Gaza strip and Khan Younis are bombarded. Israeli troops kill a leader of Jihad and six Hamas officials. Because of this, Hamas, the al-Aqsa Brigades and Jihad fire rockets into Israel. Until then, Hamas fully observed the ceasefire. Jihad and the al-Aqsa Brigades state that the ceasefire will not prevent them from reacting to Israeli violations of the agreement. In spite of this, Hamas wants to continue the ceasefire and asks Egypt for mediation.

5th November: The Gaza Strip is completely sealed off. Even food, medicine, fuel, spare parts for generators and water pumps, paper, telephones and shoes can no longer, or only in minimal amounts, enter the Gaza Strip.

8th November: Israeli bulldozers enter into the strip at several points. This leads to armed clashes with the units of the DFLP.

9th November: Hamas Chief Ismail Haniyeh declares to European delegates, who had through the sea blockade with a boat of the Free Gaza movement and visited Gaza, that Hamas could live with a solution of the Palestine problem on the basis of UN Resolutions. (Source: Ma'an 9.11.2008)

11th November: Third successful trip to Gaza on board the *Dignity*, carrying members of the European Parliament and Amira Hass, the Israeli journalist.

12th November: A further four Hamas members are killed. Israeli airplanes fire rockets at residential areas. The Palestinian factions are getting ever more skeptical about the ceasefire. Israeli bulldozers cut a 150-meter swath into an area in the

Gaza Strip for military patrols, destroying about 750 hectares of agrarian land. (Source: Ma'an 21.11.2008)

13th November: Israeli border patrols bar a UN food convoy from passing the border. The DFLP claims that for Israel this was not about the ceasefire, but about breaking resistance to the occupation. In the following days, the PFLP, the DFLP, the Popular Committees and Hamas fire projectiles at Israeli places while Israeli airplanes bomb the north of the Gaza Strip.

16th November: The Israeli Minister of Transport calls for killing the whole Hamas leadership. During new attacks, another four members of the Popular Committees are killed. By now, fifteen people have been killed during the air strikes in recent days. The Popular Committees declare the end of the cease fire. Their spokesperson blames Israel.

17th November: The DFLP and Jihad fire rockets into Israel.

18th November: The food crisis gets worse and worse. Fifty percent of the bakeries cannot operate anymore due of lack of flour. Others use animal feed to bake bread. Israeli tanks enter the strip; there are armed clashes with the PFLP and the Mujahaddin, another resistance group of Fatah.

The Israeli Navy arrests fifteen fishermen and three foreign solidarity activists off the coast of Gaza. The "Internationals" accompanied the fishermen in the hope that their presence would guarantee a minimum of protection. They are taken to Israel and get expelled after six days of solitary confinement. (Source Ma'an 18.11.2008). The three fishing boats were given back after nine days, but one boat was damaged, the GPS device was missing. During their days in prison, the solidarity workers were barred from contacting their lawyers.

http://www.freegaza.org/de/home/56-news/547-three-palestinian-fishing-boats-returned
http://www.freegaza.org/de/home/56-news/558-kidnapped-in-gaza

20th November: Yet again, a Hamas member is killed by targeted rocket strikes. Hamas increasingly comes under pressure from the other groups as well as their own base, who demand they force Israel to keep to the ceasefire. But how?

23rd November: Diplomatic sources claim that the Egyptians stepped in and got Hamas and the Israeli government to agree to resume the ceasefire according to the conditions originally negotiated. This is confirmed by Hamas. Hamas spokesman Ayman Taha furthermore states that the other resistance groups also agree to the continuation of the cease fire on the condition that the blockade is lifted. Israel does not comment on this.

24th November: A member of the Popular Committee is killed by an Israeli rocket. After Israeli claims that rockets were fired, (but no one claimed responsibility for that), the Israeli Minister of Defense Barak retracts the order to open the border for urgently needed food deliveries. As far back as August, rockets had been fired on several occasions from the Gaza Strip to the Negev desert, without claim of responsibility, which led to the closure of the border each time. At the time, Hamas leader Mahmud al-Zahhar accused Israeli agents of creating a pretext for a land invasion. (Source Ma'an 12.9.2008). Also at the time, the names of groups nobody in Gaza had heard of before and knew anything about crop up such as Ahrar al-Jalil, Tawhid Brigades or Hisb Allah. Some believe they are collaborators wanting to corrupt the ceasefire. Other voices believe they are small radical cells that think Hamas have made too many concessions.

28th November: The Israeli army kills a man from Khan Younis, who doesn't belong to any organization. On the same day, eight Israeli soldiers are injured at a boarder border post through attacks by the Mujahaddin.

30th November: Jihad declares they no longer feel bound by the ceasefire. The al-Aqsa Brigades fire projectiles at Sderot again. Hamas and Jihad are warned by mediators from Qatar

243

that Israel plans a major military offensive in the Gaza Strip. The political leadership of Hamas issues an urgent appeal to armed groups, including their own al-Qassam Brigades, to stop firing rockets into Israel.

2nd December: Israeli tanks enter the Gaza Strip again. Two teenagers are killed in air strikes.

4th December: Al-Aqsa Brigades fire rockets at Ashkelon.

5th December: Massive assaults by Jewish settlers on Palestinians in Hebron. The al-Aqsa Brigades, the PFLP and the al-Quds Brigades of the Jihad fire rockets at Israeli places as a reaction to the events in the West Bank.

7th December: A boat from Israel with peace activists wanting to bring food and gifts for children to Gaza on the occasion of the feast of sacrifice is forced to turn back by Israeli warships. The same fate befalls a boat from Qatar and another one from Libya, both of which want to deliver food to Gaza.

11th December: Forth trip to Gaza on board the *Dignity*, with activists who were remaining in Gaza to work. Called the "Student Delegation, " the boat brought out 11 Palestinian students who had visas to attend European universities and had been denied the right to leave.

13th December: Tzipi Livni states that in case a Palestinian state is set up, the Palestinian people living in Israel would be expatriated. By now, no organization thinks there is any purpose in extending the ceasefire. Brigades of the PFLP, al-Aqsa, the Popular Committees and Jihad fire at Israeli places on a regular basis. The political leadership of Hamas in Gaza, especially the de facto Prime Minister Haniyeh, has no means of preventing this, because even their own armed faction, the al-Qassam Brigades, no longer see any sense in the ceasefire.

14th December: The Hamas leadership abroad states through Khaled Mashaal that Hamas rejects an extension of the ceasefire, whereas Haniyeh still hopes that Egyptian mediation will help achieve an extension.

19th December: On the same day the six-month-ceasefire ends, all factions declare at separate mass events that they consider the ceasefire to be finished—even Fatah.

20th December: Fawzi Barhum, the spokesman of Hamas, calls on all factions to form a common resistance front. His acerbic reply to the Russian demand that Hamas should consider the extension of the ceasefire is that the onus was now on the international community to put pressure on Israel to cease the attacks on the Palestinian people, instead of blaming the victims of these attacks. (Source: Ma'an 21.12.2008)

23rd December: The former Minister of Foreign Affairs of the Hamas government, Mahmud al-Zahhar, declares once again that Hamas is prepared to continue with the ceasefire agreement, provided Israel adheres to the conditions agreed in June, in particular, the lifting of the blockade. But the discourse of al-Qassam Brigades is more subdued. Abu Ubaida, spokesman of al-Qassam Brigades, speaks only about the possibility of suspending the military action and no longer about a ceasefire and does not exclude any military action in Israel if Israel does not stop its aggression against Gaza. (Source: Ma'an 23.12.2008)

24th December: The fifth and final last voyage of the Free Gaza movement boat, the *Dignity,* arrives safely with members of a charity from Bahrain.

27th December-18th January 2009: The Israeli military attacks the Gaza Strip, killing over 1,360 people, mostly civilians, including more than 400 children. Many thousands are injured and made homeless. Israel uses phosphorus as a weapon, turns over a cemetery, shoots at the UN, schools, mosques etc. Thirteen people die on the Israeli side; four of them killed by their own soldiers in "friendly fire" incidents. The West puts the whole blame for the catastrophe on Hamas. For more information, please see:
http://www.freegaza.org/en/home/56-news/768-gaza-chronology-june-19-december-27-2008-

Appendix C: Free Gaza Related Sources

Books

Arrigoni, Vittorio, *Gaza Ratiamo Umani*, Il Manifesto-Manifestolibri, 2009 - *Gaza: Stay Human*, New York, Kube Publishing Ltd, 2010; (Available in Italian and in English)

   Bayoumi, Moustafa, editor, *Midnight on the Mavi Marmara*, New York, O/R Books, 2010; www.orbooks.com/our-books/midnight

   Goffeng, Espen, *Doedelig Farvann* (*Deadly Seas*-Available in Norwegian), Manifest Publishing, November 2010

   Jasiewicz, Ewa, *Gaza Getto Nieujarzmione*, WAB Press; Due to be published, Autumn, 2010 (Available in Polish)

   Lock, Sharyn and Sarah Irving, *Gaza Beneath the Bombs*, London, Pluto Press, 2010.

   Wright, Col. Ann and Susan Dixon, Dissent: *Voices of Conscience-Government Insiders Speak Out Against the War in Iraq*, Maui, Hawaii, Koa Books, 2010

DVDs

To Gaza with Love: Aki Nawaz, PalestineOnlineStore.com

   Gaza: We are Coming, Directed by: Yorgos Avgeropoulos, Yiannis Karipidis.A Small Planet production for Al Jazeera Satellite Network © 2009 / World Sales: Anastasia Skoubri info@smallplanet.gr; Winner of the 12th Thessaloniki Documentary Film Festival

   To Shoot an Elephant: A documentary by Alberto Acre and Mohammad Rujailah, http://toshootanelephant.com/node

Web Sites

www.palsolidarity.org, www.freegaza.org, www.witnessgaza.com, www.freedomsailors.com

Alphabetical Index